> *If you only have a hammer, you tend to see every problem as a nail*
>
> *Abraham Maslow*

COPYRIGHT

Edition one. e-ployment
March 2014
Published by UP THERE, EVERYWHERE
More information at:
www.upthereeverywhere.com
info@upthereeverywhere.com

Copyright© 2014 Julian Stubbs
All text and design©Copyright Julian Stubbs
All rights reserved. No part of this publication may be reproduced, stored in a retrieval system, or transmitted in any form or by any means electronic, mechanical, photocopying, recording or otherwise without prior permission of the author.

LEGAL DISCLAIMER

All opinions expressed in this book are those of the author alone.

The use of any term, trademark, or service mark shall not be regarded as affecting the validity of any trademark or service mark. No association between a mark owner and the author, publisher, or this work is implied. The use of any marks herein shall not be construed in any way to state, suggest, or imply, either expressly or implicitly, the promotion or disparagement of any mark or its rightful owner. The use and reproduction of any marks contained in this work and hereafter are used for "fair use" and illustrative purposes only, in the sense of describing brands or branding concepts.

To discuss branding concepts in a meaningful way, one must exemplify the subject matter and related topics with exemplary well-known brands - such as those presented and discussed herein. Accordingly, any and all trademarks and service marks are reproduced solely for descriptive purposes, and are being used without permission. The publication of any trademark or servicemark is not authorized by, associated with, or sponsored by the trademark owners. Any inadvertent omission to credits and acknowledgements can be rectified in future editions.
ISBN-13: 978-1494306861

Senior designer: Peter Langer
Senior writing advisor: David Holzer

SOURCES & REFERENCES

A list of sources and references for material used in this book is available from the publishers upon request.

ACKNOWLEDGEMENTS

I'm indebted to more people than I can possibly remember for helping me put this book together. Peter Langer, a brilliant art director, who has worked on the design and always inspires me with his ideas, thinking and is the king of type. David Holzer, who helped me write it, and Eric Dowell, my business partner for many years.

All my friends and members of the UP community and finally, my wife, boys and dog for simply being themselves.

JSS in March 2014.

e-ployment

Living and working in the cloud:
a personal journey

By Julian Stubbs

Contents

Why this book now?	6
Prologue: July 4th, 2009	9
A brief CV	12
Interview with Lynne Franks	24
Employment	28
Interview with Marga Hoek	36
Self-employment	38
Interview with Netsize	50
One way or another?	52
Interview with Kate Adams	60
Dog feed dog	62
Interview with Dag Ulrik Kühle-Gotovac, Nobel Institute	69
1984 and beyond	72
Interview with Rob England	84
Community	86
Interview with Simon Cohen	96
The time bandit. *By Eric Dowell*	100
Interview with a corporate home worker, who wished to remain anonymous. So let's just call him Brian	109
Work, life and balance	110
Interview with Nikola Tramontana	118
ME ME ME and self-responsibility	120
Interview with Stanley Bing	130
Creative Spaces	132
Interview with Ulrika Bergenkrans	142
Epilogue: July 4th, 2013	144
Sources	146

Why this book now?

The world is changing rapidly. Things seem to be converging more and more as our personal and work lives become increasingly intermingled. Today, we think nothing of watching a fun, viral, video on YouTube at ten o'clock in the morning or answering business emails at ten at night. Work and life have become blurred. This is the picture for many of us who work in service industries. Traditional employment is fast becoming a thing of the past. But where will it lead next?

The aftershocks of the financial crisis are profoundly affecting the way governments and corporations, that have long been the main sources of traditional employment, are now viewing today's workforce. If we have a safety net at all, it has holes that are growing larger all the time. We're being encouraged to become more independent so that we don't cost governments so much money.

Corporations are shedding us and outsourcing so that they can save money and earn more for their shareholders. In this scenario, we have little choice as to whether or not we become independent.

If we become successfully self-employed and work in the cloud, we are then faced with the challenge of finding the right work-life balance. But, we're told, the consequences of failing to our get our work-life balance right can have disastrous effects on our well-being and our families. We're also in danger of becoming isolated and lonely without an office to go to and a water cooler to gather around. So there are issues in entering this brave new world.

But there is a third way of working, and that is ultimately what this book is about. I know it works because I'm one of its pioneers. I say this simply because it's true. I don't necessarily have any more insight than anyone else. However, along with a small group of other people, I arrived at this way of working out of necessity, and not because I wanted to build an empire. (Although I have to say that a modest global empire is quietly building itself.)

We've written this short book to give you our take on how employment in the creative services industry, and possibly the whole service industry itself, could be impacted by new business models such as ours. We call our model E-Ployment. It paints a picture of the world beyond traditional employment, enabled by the cloud, digital tools and a hybrid of remote working. E-Ployees will increasingly form and work in highly connected "global communities". They will often derive their income from multiple sources and will certainly be more focussed on achieving a healthy work–life balance. They are also people concerned with the environment and there are some big upsides there as well, as fewer people will need to face a daily commute.

We're a small company with a big idea. I wrote this book because I wanted to share that idea with others. I know that working anywhere and everywhere in the cloud offers a huge amount of freedom and massive benefits for people like us and like our clients. This book talks about employment, self-employment and introduces the third new way – E-Ployment.

Prologue

July 4th, 2009

It was the Fourth of July, 2009. Independence Day for Americans, but for me it was my wedding anniversary. A little ironic, I guess, as being a Brit I had married an American. I'd always argued that the British, under good King George (who was unfortunately a few cards short of a full stack) hadn't so much lost America as misplaced it. Anyway, my act of marrying an American on Independence Day was firstly a very easy way to remember my wedding anniversary and secondly, in my own little way, a means of taking America back again, one piece at a time.

My wife Anne and I always enjoying throwing a good party to celebrate Independence Day, and we were determined that this was a Fourth of July our neighbours in the small Swedish town just outside of Stockholm, where we lived, were not going to forget.

With the annual celebration due to kick off soon, the barbeque sizzled. There was plenty of wine and champagne on ice, and anything else our guests might conceivably want. Waiters and waitresses in crisp white shirts darted from table to table making sure everything looked perfect. The sounds of jazz drifted down from the house to our lower garden.

I stood on our deck, looked up at the blue sky, empty but for a fading vapour trail, and then across the shining water of the lake to the forest beyond. The white sail of a yacht drifted into view.

I was in paradise, or as close to it as I'd ever come. I had a wonderful wife and two great sons, lived in a beautiful house in probably one of the most desirable parts of Sweden, and my family was part of a community of people we were proud to call our friends.

Right then, I should have been raising a glass of champagne and toasting my good fortune. But something was wrong with this picture.

Ironically enough, it was all about independence. I was employed by an international marketing communications company to head up global branding, which meant plenty of money and a life that was as good as it gets in most respects. I was earning in a month what some people earn in a year. But, at the same time, I felt more trapped than at any other time in my life.

"Everything looking good"?, Niki, the husband half of the catering team we'd hired asked, standing next to me. "Going to be a great party".

"I'm sure it will be", I said, "thanks for all your help".

"You don't sound convincing", said Niki.

I looked at him. His powers of observation seemed pretty sharp.

"Actually", I said, trusting my instincts that he seemed more than your average waiter, 'I'm feeling that things aren't exactly right".

"Something I can help fix", he said quizzically looking around at the food and drinks that were laid out.

"Nothing to do with the party – you've done a great job", I replied. "Just life".

He looked at me long and hard and replied, "Actually, that's something I might be able to help fix as well". He dipped his hand into his pocket and pulled out a business card. His name was on it, but underneath it said Personal Life Coach.

"The catering is a side line", he smiled. "You look like you need to consider your life balance a bit more", he said. "Give me a call". With that he was off attending to some guests who had arrived.

★ ★ ★

The sun was setting. It was now just after ten o'clock the same evening. "Looks like it's going to be a beautiful day tomorrow", I said.

Anne turned to me and raised her glass of champagne to mine. We touched glasses. "It's going to have to be outstanding to be better than today", she said. "Happy Fourth of July, darling".

"Same to you", I said. I was deeply tired but, for a change, it was a pleasant kind of exhaustion.

"Niki did a great job – everything went as planned".

"He's certainly a good person to know", I said.

"What an amazing stroke of luck that we found him when we did", Anne said.

"I'm not sure if it was luck", I said. I slipped my hand into my pocket and found the business card Niki had given me and looked at it. Personal Life Coach. The words jumped out at me.

"Come on", Anne said. "Let's dance".

★ ★ ★

A month later I was in Niki's office, at the gym he ran, and I was waiting for his verdict on my health. It felt a little like being in the headmaster's office back in the day when they were really scary. On the other side of the glass door people worked out, mostly with an air of grim determination. The thump of upbeat music mixed with the clank of weights being dropped and the occasional grunt.

I think you know what I'm going to tell you", Niki said. I nodded. "But I don't think you know how serious it is. If you continue on the way you are", Niki said, "it's not going to be good". I looked at him, swallowed hard... "You're not the healthiest man I've ever met. You're overweight and seriously out of condition. I don't think I need to spell it out for you, do I"?

"No", I said, "you don't. So, what do I do"?

"I can help you", Niki said. "But it's really up to you".

"I want to change", I said. "I need help".

As I slipped behind the wheel of my car half an hour later and eased out into the traffic, *We Can Work It Out* by The Beatles became *Yesterday*. I smiled at the obvious symbolism but, on that Friday afternoon in Sweden in 2009, I began to think back over my life. How had I become what I was?

> *Life is like riding a bicycle, To keep your balance, you must keep moving*
>
> Albert Einstein

Chapter #1
A brief CV

I wanted me
as my

BOSS

e-ployment

I have always disliked the word "employment". It's heavy and ugly and, for me, conjures up a depressing picture. I think of high desks, quill pens, ankles in chains. Which is probably why I've been so driven to be my own boss: to employ my self.

But don't worry, this isn't my life story. I just want to start by giving you some background, so you can understand why I'm such a passionate believer in working anywhere and everywhere and being e-ployed.

* * *

While I was at college, I worked on a market stall selling fruit. This taught me more about marketing than any other job I've ever done. I learnt that display is key. All those pyramids of apples are there for a reason. I discovered how to attract an audience by doing something sensational: juggling bananas, in my case. I also learned how to use language to draw people in by developing what we called a "patter", a script to sell my product. Most importantly, I learnt how to count cash accurately.

But I was outside in all weather, I had to be up at the crack of dawn and I was often cold, wet and tired.

* * *

My first job after I graduated college was selling advertising space for a newspaper in Oxford. After three days I realised I was pretty useless at selling ads. The next morning, in my tiny bedsit (so small I called it a "sit-sit") I reached out of bed to the sink, made myself a cup of tea and decided to talk to my boss, the fearsome Norman.

"Norman", I said as I stormed politely into his office, "I'm terrible at selling ads and I won't last. What shall we do"?

Rather than throw me out on my ear, Norman sat back in his swivel chair, eyed me through narrowed eyes and said: "This may surprise you son, but I actually admire your honesty". Norman put me with one of the top sales guys to learn how he did it. My performance improved and I stayed for a year.

I had learned three things: first that I didn't like having a boss. Second, that when things are looking bad and you are feeling worried about a situation, the best thing is to accept the very worst that can happen (in this case that Norman would fire me) and then confront it head on and deal with the consequences. It's far better than letting it drag on and live a worried existence. Finally, I had learned that I wanted a boss who was caring, smart and had my best interests at heart. A boss who would also allow me to be well rewarded. Who would let me drive whatever company car I wanted. In other words, I wanted me as my boss.

Actually, I saw myself as chief executive officer of the most important company in the world from a very early age. That company was yours truly: Julian Stubbs Inc.

I was responsible for earning money and selling *me* to clients. This meant product development, marketing and deciding how my product (moi) should look in the market place. When I was younger, the most important thing was employee health – mental and physical. Mine.

Mind you, I lost sight of that last bit. But more on that later.

* * *

My first job in advertising was with a great little ad agency in Cheltenham, a town about 100 miles west of London. From there I become marketing manager of a company working with aluminium. After a big-name UK advertising agency offered me a better job, the aluminium company offered me lots of money, a cash bonus and a promotion to become head of marketing for the whole group, reporting directly to the CEO.

I knew I should move on and not take the bribe but... I took the promotion, stayed, and had a very pleasant year before heading off to Sweden for the first time. I learned that it's great to take a risk, but only when you're as sure as you can be that the time is right and you have as much of a financial cushion as possible.

* * *

I took a huge risk moving to Sweden when I didn't know the language or the client base. In any case, six months after I arrived, the advertising agency I had taken a job with went belly up. I had no choice but to head back to London and go out on my own. I discovered that I didn't like being an employee who was at the mercy of other people's bad business decisions. I really didn't.

A couple of great things came out of my first Swedish adventure. First of all, I discovered I loved the country. Everything worked. Whatever class of hotel you stayed in, the shower functioned. Unlike in Britain, central heating and triple-glazing meant it never got cold in Swedish houses in winter.

And Sweden was fair. I'll give you an example. In British companies at that time there were often three cafeterias: one for management, another for white-collar workers and the last one for manual workers. In Sweden everyone ate in one restaurant, and often I'd eat at the same table as the CEO and a caretaker. Both had shared values and lived different versions of the same life. There appeared to be no "them" and "us".

The second great outcome of my time in Sweden was I met Eric Dowell.

By now it was the late 1980s. Back in London and looking for a job, I got a call from one of my oldest friends named Philip. He'd just left, a big ad agency called Allen Brady & Marsh for getting into a punch up with the creative director – not a career-enhancing move.

Somehow, the British *Daily Mail* newspaper picked up on what had happened. Not surprisingly, they made up a story about how the punch up was over an argument about creative strategy for the Conservative Party account, which ABM had at the time. Philip, who is nothing short of a genius as an advertising man, was not the tallest of people however so the *Daily Mail* had nicknamed him Mighty Mouse.

Philip was convinced the story had blown his chances of ever working in advertising again and was distraught. He kept calling me for advice on what he should do. I had no idea and, in any case, I was worried about my own future. One night when Philip called, to shut him up more than anything else, I said: "Why don't you start your own agency and call it Mighty Mouse"? We finished the call.

A week later, Philip called again. "Guess what", he said. "I took your advice".
"What advice"?
"You know, to start an agency called Mighty Mouse. So, I've done it and I've put you down as one of the owners. What do you think"?
"Um. I'll get back to you".
Five minutes later I called Philip back. "Why not"? I said. "I'm in".

We needed a creative director and I immediately thought of Eric Dowell. Eric was, and still is, an American. He had been creative director at the advertising agency I had worked at in Sweden that had gone bankrupt. He was tall, spoke English like Dick van Dyke, and seemed to exist on pizza. Eric was up for joining us in London, and so we started Mighty Mouse Communications: three guys and one of the first Apple Macintosh computers to arrive in London.

So began my love affair with Apple and my realisation that being an early adopter of technology can really shape the success of a communications company. (I still have the first Mac Classic I ever owned. It was a beautiful piece of design, even if it looks like a 1950s television to me now.)

Like any start-up, Mighty Mouse was a giant leap into the unknown, but we hit the ground running. Our first client was HMV Record Stores, shortly thereafter we worked on projects for Beefeater Gin. Within a year, there were ten of us, and I was a boss for the first time.

Did I like being a boss? I wasn't sure. I loved being part of a shared vision and I got a huge kick out of building a business. It felt right to sell myself, my company and work that I was genuinely proud of without having to bend the truth. But I wasn't keen on having to tell people what to do or being responsible for their livelihoods - or in fact their lives.

Because of my contacts from my time abroad, we began to get business from Sweden, so I persuaded my partners to let me set up a Swedish branch of Mighty Mouse.

Things went rather smoothly from the word go. However, I do remember a morning during which I discovered just how lost in translation things can really get. We were making a presentation to the CEO of a Swedish multinational and had been ushered into the ultra-posh boardroom where we waited like school boys in the headmasters study.

The CEO sat at the end of a table the size of an aircraft carrier. He was a giant – the size of a small house. Even though I was several metres away from him at my end of the table, when I stood up he still seemed to tower over me, nostrils like shotgun barrels.

We put the first board up on an easel. It had the Mighty Mouse logo on it. He looked at it, smirked and asked "So who's the big cheese"? The dozen or so people from his exec team laughed at his little joke. The presentation went well, but the CEO and his team smirked all the way through.

As we were being escorted from the building I said to one of the junior aides "What was so funny"?

He turned to me. "In Swedish, Mighty Mouse means giant pussy".

A week later they appointed us as their main agency, which taught me that actually a little bit of humour is not a bad thing. We kept the name Mighty Mouse and prospered.

A year later, we were employing 20 people in Sweden, just as we were in London. Once again, I was the boss, but it still wasn't exactly my cup of tea.

I left Mighty Mouse two years later to become vice president of a large multinational biotech company in Sweden. My role was global and I had a staff of 30 (sigh). Not surprisingly, I spent most of my time dealing with staff issues, which wasn't my idea of fun. Although I promised myself I'd leave after three years I ended up staying five, moving on, happily, after a company merger.

Now I definitely knew I didn't like being a boss or manager. To me, management isn't a good thing. I actually can't stand the word. It's non-productive.

* * *

Next I became a freelance consultant. I thought: "Finally, I have the freedom to do what I love on my own terms". In my case, this meant the freedom to work really hard all the time. But all my hard work paid off, and soon I was making more money than I'd ever made in my life.

So, in work terms, I had it all. But I was lonely and this took me by surprise. I didn't like offices or much to do with them. But offices meant being around other people and I didn't want to be on my own all day. It wasn't just that I wanted someone to gossip or go to lunch with. A large part of my work was about coming up with great ideas and, to be honest, I always liked bouncing ideas off of others first. And a major part of why I love what I do is being around really good people who stimulate, provoke and challenge me. I'm my own worst enemy when I'm alone too much.

I missed people like Eric. I missed the agency buzz. So six months later I bought myself back into Mighty Mouse, became CEO, and we changed our name to Dowell Stubbs. After a somewhat rocky beginning, which meant we had to lay off some people (a part of being the boss that made me feel terrible), we began to do well – in fact very well. Within six years we were large, by Stockholm standards, with 40 employees, and we had offices in the flashy part of the city. But again boredom set in, as well as dissatisfaction with being a boss. Within six months of feeling like this we decided to sell out to a global communications agency.

I stayed on as head of Branding at the company that had acquired us and Eric became their Creative Director in New York. My role was global once again and I was being extremely well paid. Which brings us to where this story started: Independence Day, 2009.

★ ★ ★

March, three years later, and I was walking in New York's Madison Square Park with Eric, kicking our way through dead leaves. I was in NY for a client meeting. Eric turned to me, cleared his throat and said: "This isn't fun anymore, is it? And I don't mean walking in the park on a freezing cold day".

I knew exactly what Eric meant. Since we teamed up and I'd gotten used to his eccentricities we've always had a kind of telepathy. It's one of the reasons we work so well together. "No", I said. "It isn't. So what are we going to do about it"?

We strolled over to a bench and sat down. "Why do we even have to be here"? Eric said. "I mean, you'd have thought that with net, broadband and whatever, there would be no need to get on a plane and go anywhere".

"I like getting on planes", I said. "But I know what you mean. We could be at home right now having this conversation on video chat".

"So, why aren't we"?

"What do you mean"?

"Like I said, why are we even here"?

"Do you mean: why aren't we freelancers working remotely..."?

"I dislike that word", Eric said. "Intensely".

"So do I. But you know what I mean. And you know why I don't like being freelance. It's precisely because it's too lonely. What I don't understand is why no one has thought of taking the online community model and applying it to business. Creating something totally new. A new business model".

Eric looked up at the clear blue sky over Manhattan and down at me. "That's not a bad idea", he said. He looked at his watch. "Meeting in five minutes. Need to get back".

I stood up, a vicious gust of icy wind took my breath away. I hunched my shoulders and turned into the wind.

"We could be meeting on video chat too", I muttered.

* * *

Back in Sweden, a month or so later, on a spring day that was almost warm, Eric and I took another walk in a park.

"I really do hate this", I said.

"But it's a lovely day in Stockholm", Eric said. "The sap is rising, spring is in the air." He nodded at a young couple, clearly head over heels in love. "What's not to like"?

"No", I said. "I can't stand the way we're working. It took me almost two hours to drive into the city this morning. It should take 45 minutes. And that two hours is totally dead, non-productive time. Not to mention the waste of fuel and the pollution".

"What do you mean"?

"Exhaust fumes".

"You could always buy a smaller, more fuel-efficient car".

"That's not the point. It's just totally unnecessary. We don't need to be here. We could be at home".

"You said you didn't want to do that again. Working...'remotely'", Eric said, making air quotation marks with his fingers.

"Just because we're not working in an office, it doesn't mean that we have to be cut off from people. Why can't we use the whole online community thing to build a business? Of people like us"?

"I don't know", Eric said. "Why can't we"?

I looked at a pair of teenagers making a goodbye kiss last forever. "I think we're going to resign", I said. "We can't do this anymore. Life is too short".

***

Now you have probably picked up that I love what I do. I'm driven, I probably am a bit of an empire-builder as well as an early adopter. I want to be my own boss but no one else's, I need to be around other people and feel part of something, but I love being alone when I need to as well. Added to this I really want to make a difference.

***

One other thing. I have always believed in making life happen rather than wait for it to happen to me. I've always embraced change. Apart from jumping before I was pushed, I truly believe that an easy life isn't good for me - or anyone. It takes away my edge.

So, you could say that, on top of everything else, I'm still hungry. But maybe that's the diet Niki's got me on.

> *To live is the rarest thing in the world. Most people exist, that is all*
>
> — *Oscar Wilde*

e-ployment

Interview with Lynne Franks
by David Holzer, UP member

Lynne Franks, recognised as the UK's leading women's empowerment guru, is a successful business woman, author, broadcaster, speaker and futurist. An acclaimed international spokesperson and advisor on the changes in today's and tomorrow's world, Lynne has throughout her career created and promoted many new initiatives that have led the way in shifts in society.

One of Lynne's paradigm-shifting enterprises is B.Hive, a new kind of business club and feminine space where like-minded women can come together to network and share their stories. For women who want a space to have meetings, catch up with emails and hold events, B.Hive offers a stylish, professional environment.

Lynne is always in tune with and often ahead of the zeitgeist. This makes her an ideal person to talk to about the changing nature of employment in the twenty-first century, partly driven by the cloud.

* * *

Lynne, do you see the nature of freelance employment changing?
Absolutely. The independent freelance creatives coming in to B.Hive, my women's business lounges, see themselves as independent entrepreneurs, not just self-employed freelancers. They've started their own businesses, even if their business is them and their own ideas, capabilities and skills.

They use B.Hive, other business lounges or coffee shops for meetings once or twice a week and work from their kitchen tables at home. In many cases, they're not interested in employing people and growing in size, perhaps because they've come from the corporate world. When they have a project that needs other people to create a team, they'll find them through their networks, in a place like B.Hive, or through their own online networks. But they all still see themselves as independent.

What's interesting, certainly in the UK, is that these independent operators working in this kind of way are now mounting up to a big critical mass, creating a fair amount of revenue and having quite an effect on the economy.

Do you feel this way of working has something to offer women that it doesn't offer men?
I think that style of working is for men and women, actually, because men are just as keen to stay at home these days and work around their children as are women.

What about the corporate world and remote working?
Because of developments in technology we now have the choice in the sophisticated Western world of working in a different way. Flexible and remote working is the way forward. Having big expensive offices in central venues and commuting is a thing of the past. More and more of the big companies I work with have their teams working at home, coming together for meetings online. Technology is also enabling people to work as individuals within a large company. I think an entrepreneurial spirit – being creative, breaking rules, being passionate generally about what you do - is just as evident in people working in big companies - as it is in people starting businesses. A lot more companies are now looking for individuals with entrepreneurial style, particularly these new, younger technology companies, such as Google and Facebook.

Do you think that age has any relevance to that entrepreneurial spirit?
Not really. In fact the 60+ age group in the UK is where a huge amount of new business owners are coming from. There are lots of older people becoming entrepreneurs who perhaps did work in the corporate world or for large companies for a number of years. Now, instead of being retired, they're going into some kind of entrepreneurial role.

Let's talk about UP. Could you see a cloud-based marketing services company like UP, made up of individual entrepreneurs working as an online community business, taking on big, multinational agencies at their own game?

It's already happening. I've heard of people in the States and Europe taking on the big ad agencies by coming together as a creative team or as the best team for whatever the project is. For a client, all they need to know is that there's somebody who is responsible and they only have to pay through one person and not 12. If you set things up so it's easy and convenient for the client they'll definitely look at going down that route. Because they know they're not having to commit to an ad agency and they might actually be getting some better creative work. Ad agencies and marketing service companies should be extremely wary right now of the freelance networks that are going out to compete with them.

Even with PR, which is my background, if I were starting now I would have a whole series of smart people I knew I could work with well, who had the same values, and I'd build up an independent team of creative freelancers and pitch for different things.

So you don't think big name advertising agencies count for as much?

Less and less. In any case, it's individual creatives who win the awards.

A major aspect of UP's vision is doing good in the real world. Why do you think there's a movement in business today to want to make a difference?

It's been building up for a long time, and people are aware now that they can't really trust government to do it. We have to make a difference ourselves. We now know what's going on in the world through social media and technology, and we didn't before, and we can see that we might live really well in the West, but there are a lot of people suffering elsewhere. We want to help. It's a natural human instinct for most humans – to want to help others. If we can do it through our work, all the better.

You're a futurist. How do you see the immediate future of business?

My instincts tell me that we're going to see far more small businesses using technology, working at the community level with systems like local digital currency. There will be a far more inclusive perspective on businesses being part of your life rather than running your life. That whole work-life balance thing is going to become an essential part of how you plan your life now.

How do you feel about your own work-life balance?

As we're sitting here in Mallorca on the terrace with the sun shining, the sky and sea as blue as blue, I'd say it's going pretty well really. I'm quite happy with my work-life balance because I choose what I want to do most of the time. In some ways I was a bit of a pioneer in deciding how I want to live my life and just going for it. That's the other thing about people starting their own small businesses. They don't want to be told how to live their lives.

What do you see as the potential for working online in areas that are specifically of interest to you, which are women and the Third World?

I see it in terms of time, communication, teaching and learning. I'm personally looking at the whole area of online learning – teaching women confidence, how to start a business, how to be sustainable - by using technology in a very smart way. And it's all mobile focused. Everyone's got a mobile phone now.

Here's an example: solar-operated tablets are being used to train women in Afghanistan to make jewelery. This is changing these women's lives so they have an income and can work from home, making beautiful products that will bring in a revenue stream to their community. It's just mind-blowing really, these miracles in technology.

This is a very exciting time to bring together real-time learning and peer support circles. It's the start of a new paradigm that will allow things to happen that we haven't even touched on yet. They will probably happen first in some of the third world countries and Africa because the mobile phone industry has focused on services for local entrepreneurs in those regions.

What is your vision for your work with women?
I'm working with women at the highest level of leadership and at the grass roots level so we can truly become equal with men. So we can create a new, peaceful, healthy, sustainable way of living for every single person on the planet. In a way that doesn't exploit the environment. All these things are what we want. I believe we have the tools to make them happen, and technology is a very big part of that.

And are you optimistic for the future?
I'm very optimistic as long as I don't look at the news too often. It's also the only way forward. I believe we have to be optimistic, otherwise there's no future. Don't you?

A brief CV

> *Never complain of that of which it is at all times in your power to rid yourself*

Adam Smih,
The Theory of Moral Sentiments

Chapter #2

Employment

EMPLOYMENT EMPLOYMENT EMPLOYMENT

EMPLOYMENT EMPLOYMENT EMPLOYMENT

For me, it comes down to making a distinction between employment and work. But before we get into that and what it means to me, let's look at a brief history of work and the attitudes to it that have shaped the way most of us, certainly my generation, see work and being employed. (1)

* * *

The Greeks called work *ponos*, which means sorrow. This will strike a chord with those people in life who still get Monday morning blues when the alarm goes off. Personally, I'm an obsessively early riser and up most days at 5.30 am. I will lie in on the weekends – until 6 am. I guess it's because, at age 11, I had a newspaper route that started at 6 am. Before I started I used to love to get up and play chess with my Dad, who was always up at 5 am. Anyway, back to the Greeks.

As far as they were concerned, only slaves did manual labour. Philosophers like Plato and Aristotle regarded hard work as beneath contempt. Work was for the majority who made it possible for the free minority elite to eat, drink and not freeze to death while they contemplated art, philosophy and politics. You could say things haven't changed much.

* * *

According to the eighteenth century Scottish pioneering political economist Adam Smith, money came about with the division of labour, because what labourers produced from their own work – let's say food - only met part of their needs. Something had to be created as a common medium of exchange, and so coins were introduced.

Or, in the immortal words of Groucho Marx, "While money can't buy happiness, it certainly lets you choose your own form of misery".

As usual, the Chinese got there first – they began using coins in the eleventh century BC – but it was the Greeks who put faces and figures on coins in the fifth century BC.

* * *

By the time the Middle Ages rolled around, work was still regarded as having no actual value or point, other than to keep your family and community fed and housed. What was new was the Christian ideal that work was simply part of human society, presided over by God. Also, work was seen as God's punishment for the original sin of Adam and Eve, which led to them being kicked out of paradise. Work meant not being idle. Idleness led to sin. But the money earned by working was a good thing because it kept people from relying on charity. (However, many hundreds of years later, when I was growing up, it was definitely the case that to be respectable meant having a job. Any job.)

When it comes to the Protestant Work Ethic, we have sixteenth century religious leaders Martin Luther and John Calvin to thank. Luther believed that it was possible to serve God through work, that people were born into a particular job and that changing professions was going against God's laws. To this, Calvin added the idea that choosing an occupation that made as much money as possible was an actual religious duty. You were doing the right thing by God if you changed professions, even if it was from a trade your family had practiced for generations, if you could make more money. And if you were successful, this was proof that you were one of God's Chosen.

As we know, the Protestant Work Ethic is what shaped the concept of work in much of Europe, America and beyond, and it definitely has something to do with the way I feel about -- if not work, then idleness. I wish that doing nothing didn't make me feel guilty, but it does. A good dose of Thatcherism in the 1980s probably reinforced this feeling of guilt.

With the emergence of the Industrial Revolution in the early nineteenth century, the work ethic had become less of a Protestant "value" and more about being useful. It was our social duty to work hard and avoid poverty and the evils of idleness. But now, as manual labour was being replaced by feeding a machine, it became harder for an ordinary person to improve his or her lot in life by working hard.

With the Industrial Revolution, the notion of division of labour really kicked in. Industry was perfect for dividing labour, unlike, say, agriculture. According to Adam Smith, division of labour was more responsible for an increase in production than anything else. The increase had nothing to do with some people having a stronger work ethic than others. Interestingly enough, Adam Smith also argues that the division of labour has nothing to do with some people being better at particular jobs than others or having a particular talent. It's simply a result of specialisation, and this is the product of the human need to barter.

At the same time, the *employers* who ran the factories that drove the Industrial Revolution began to impose more and more control over their *employees* to make sure they, the *employers*, could compete. Employment became about repetition over skill and the discipline needed to do the same tedious action over and over again. In factories, it was also hard to define yourself by what you did. No matter how much skill a factory job might require, there was no sense of purpose and definitely no spiritual reward, whether from God or anyone else. By the late nineteenth century, the notion of a surplus became a reality when factories produced more than could be consumed. So working hard and making lots of a product no longer meant prosperity.

As competition between factories heated up, employers became obsessed with keeping costs down at all cost. Under the traditional model of management, employees were seen as inherently lazy and motivated only by money, which meant they had to be regulated as tightly as possible. Scientific management theory arrived, which was all about specialisation and dividing jobs into simple tasks. It held that this would make workers work harder and meant that they were paid more. Scientific managers believed it all came down to money.

But there was a problem with this theory: managers realised that some people worked harder than others and didn't need as much supervision; whereas other people distrusted management when their pay didn't keep up with their improved productivity.

(Here's an interesting aside: All over the world, Manchester is associated with the colour red, and most people think this has something to do with Manchester United, my least favourite football team – I'm a Liverpool fan through and through. (That's soccer for those in the US.) But there's a far deeper connection with the red in Manchester's history. In 1845, when Engels wrote his book *The Condition of the Working Class in England*, he was describing conditions in the dark satanic mills of Manchester. Marx picked up on what Engels wrote and gave the world communism. Thanks a lot, Karl!

After World War II, behaviourist theories of management argued that workers weren't actually intrinsically lazy, they were adaptive. A boring work environment made them do less because they were, well, bored. Give workers stimulation and fulfillment and they will perform better. This is when ideas of corporate human relations began to become widespread. Company newspapers, employee awards and company social events, among other things, were used to make employees feel better about the company they worked for and the work they did. But it was still an "us" and "them" situation: employer vs. employee.

The late 1950s saw the arrival of job enrichment theories, and these triggered fundamental changes in the employer-employee relationship. Achievement, recognition, responsibility, advancement and personal growth were now seen as more important than salary, company policies, supervisory style, working conditions and relationships with fellow workers. If these were not optimal, performance was impaired, but they didn't actually motivate workers when they were present.

In 1960, a guy named McGregor introduced the concepts of theory "X", authoritarian scientific management, and theory "Y", participatory management. In participatory management, the management and workers work together towards a common goal, creating the possibility of using the work ethic as a resource within the workplace.

We're almost done but there's one other factor which has a bearing on my own personal attitude to work.

All my jobs, apart from working on the market stall, have been information age jobs and not industrial age. A typical industrial age job did not and does not involve much thought, judgment or decision-making. An information age job usually involves plenty of independent decision-making and self-responsibility, and this is where a strong work ethic is needed. If you don't have one, you simply can't make the decisions needed to keep customers satisfied and support the company employing you.

So, if you do information age work, as I always have, and like to do, the work itself becomes its own reward. It's not pain, but pleasure.

Also, obviously, there are many benefits in working for the "right" company. Apart from being well-paid and doing something you like, work is where your goals are set – if you're someone who wants to climb the ladder to the top – where you feel part of something, where you make friends and even meet your husband or wife. I did, in fact.

But, employment is only half the story.

* * *

At the start of this chapter I introduced the idea of a distinction between employment and work. When I think of employment I picture clocking in and clocking out, a boss looking over your shoulder. In my world, employment is dying or dead. Work, which is all about *self-responsibility*, lives on.

I knew from the word go that I didn't want to work for anyone else. I wanted to be *self-employed*. Self-employed people just seem to be happier and to have more fun.

And similarly, I don't particularly enjoy employing others and having to be responsible for them. It seemed to me that being a boss meant that I had to manage people in a way that didn't feel natural and actually was far less productive.

* * *

Now that we've looked at the history of conventional employment. Let's explore the unconventional. Always much more fun.

Interview with Marga Hoek
by David Holzer, UP member

UP: Wow!

Marga Hoek describes herself as "a real businesswoman, an entrepreneurial board member and someone who connects the political, science and business worlds at a strategic level".

In Holland, Marga is well-known as a figurehead of sustainable development. She's the head of the Green Business Association, chairwoman of the Green Scientists Association and a member of the World Business Council. She writes books and articles and has a high media profile that is becoming increasingly global.

Marga's book, Doing Business in the New Economy: Seven Windows on Sucess offers a clear, coherent definition and description of the New Economy that illustrates exactly how businesses operate within it. The book meets the great demand and need for insight into the positive value creation that drives the fully sustainable economy – also known as the "circular" economy. This economy – as depicted in the book – is sustainable in terms of environmental, social and financial assets.

The book takes the position that a new outlook can be truly inspiring, given that it's human nature to want to become involved in positive causes from which we all stand to benefit. That is to say, we would rather get involved for positive rather than negative reasons or out of sheer necessity.

Marga was introduced to UP by founding member Lawrence Masle and, we're delighted to say, decided to write a chapter using UP as an example of how a New Economy business can work. We asked her why.

* * *

First of all, how would you define the New Economy?

An economy built on the value of the ecological, financial and social assets that we incorporate. These are circular, sustaining each other. In the New Economy we make maximum use of all the interacting variables and use factors like connectedness, globalisation and localisation, which can speed up its scale and sustainability. I deal with this in Chapter Zero of my book.

Why UP?

UP is inspiring, and when I talk about you, people say "Wow!" UP defines the new economy. You combine interacting trends, connecting knowledge worldwide that you can deliver anywhere, and you're sustainable. What's exciting is that a single member of UP can compete against a huge company in a pitch for, say, a city marketing project, and win. Because you can draw on your global network to share knowledge about city marketing. Your perspective is far wider than that of a person within a company, enclosed by its four walls. UP is evidence that a new way of working and a conviction to be sustainable really can give you a better competitive position.

Fantastic but, playing devil's advocate, what do you see as the challenges of UP's approach?

The challenge is to find a way of communicating digitally to get people all over the world emotionally involved and get them connected. This is easier said than done. You need people who really are networkers to enable the infrastructure to come alive.

On a broader level, what do you see as the future of work for, let's say, people like us?

The New Economy is organised in networks, unlike the old economy, which was about business sectors. Networks are about "How"? and "Who with"?. They don't specify "What?". Today's successful organisations work in networks rather than hierarchical systems. It's much more interesting and productive for networks to interact with other networks. This is the shape of the future. Our businesses will be networks.

Let's look at the New Cities, for example. New Cities are network conglomerates that are geographically spread out from around original cities. They are areas that have core competencies that attract business and innovation to them. Rotterdam in the Netherlands illustrates this perfectly. Rotterdam doesn't make anything. The area's core competitive edge is that it is a hub for knowledge about how to transport anything that has to get from A to B or back again, which may need to be recycled or enriched. And, increasingly, this includes content as well as physical things. Rotterdam is distributing content all over the world.

In one sense, UP is exactly the same. You don't make anything. You distribute knowledge and content all over the world through your network. UP is helping to shape the future!

Now it's our turn to say "Wow!" Marga. Thanks.

> "*Greed, for the lack of a better word, is good*
>
> Gordon Gekko,
> Wall Street, 1987

Chapter #3

Self-employment

A

ONE MAN BAND

Remember the 1980s? This was the time when television in the UK brought us characters like Harry Enfield's Loadsamoney, a brash, loud male representing the new rich and exemplifying the idea of "if you've got it flaunt it". The same period gave us Oliver Stone's film Wall Street and the story of corporate raider Gordon Gekko who said: "Greed, for want of a better word, is good".

* * *

As is so often the case, what sounds like outrageous satire is based on truth. Gekko's speech was inspired by something Wall Street arbitrageur Ivan Boesky said in 1986 at the University of California, Berkeley's commencement ceremony. That year, Boesky had paid a $100 million penalty to settle insider trading charges. Boesky said: "Greed is all right, by the way. I want you to know that. I think greed is healthy. You can be greedy and still feel good about yourself".

And, boy, did we get greedy in the 1980s. We learnt shopping was good – remember "retail therapy"?

Rapacious consumerism fuelled the idea that a product's intrinsic value

increased greatly when the product transformed into a brand. Think about Adam Smith's belief that the "real price of every thing...is the toil and trouble of acquiring it". (How does that work when easy credit enters into the equation?)

Now, I love brands. Always have. And one of the brands I've been lucky enough to have a lifelong relationship with is Porsche. For me, it was all about the pure functionality of the car, the beautiful sound of the engine of a 911. And of course, the pared down simplicity, which probably had something to do with its connection with the Volkswagen Beetle (my first car).

Well, the 1980s almost destroyed the Porsche brand. Featured in an episode of Miami Vice, with a soundtrack of Duran Duran and Spandau Ballet, it became an icon of hedonism, selfishness and conspicuous consumption at its worst. The tarnishing of the Porsche brand encapsulates the story of the 1980s for many of us. The car manufacturer was almost dead by the mid '90s and it was only the last minute strategy of re-focusing on their roots and heritage, as well as a sorting out of severe quality and manufacturing issues, that saved them.

But there were also great things about the '80s. In the '80s, the work ethic became all about rising to the challenge, thinking for yourself, personal growth, producing great work and being recognised for this. Having fun at work. Great! This was what I'd always wanted.

For me, it was a time when my need to be master of my own destiny and to do creative work collided happily with the spirit of the times. So much so that it was only relatively recently when I began to question the factors that helped shape me, my work ethic and my lifestyle. The spirit of the age had become mine. But was that such a good thing? Many of us who lived through the '80s and succeeded because of it have been asking the same question for a while now.

In some respects I think people surrendered some essential values and rights and possibly, one could argue, even care less about democracy, provided we were all allowed to earn ever larger amounts of money and go shopping.

* * *

As we now know, the forces driving the shift towards an entrepreneurial, individualistic approach to work had been driven by the US as part of a larger economic, social and political agenda since at least the early 1970s.

In 1971, American president Richard Nixon took the US off the gold standard, disconnecting paper money from reality. Western Europe followed his lead. UK banking reform and deregulation of the finance industry began. Shiny, seductive credit cards were introduced, and the amount of credit available to consumers grew enormously. Today, many will argue that the deregulation of finance led directly to the global financial crisis of 2007/2008, which still plagues Western Europe and the rest of the world.

With more readily available credit came a huge increase in consumer debt; hence, people had to work more to pay it off. So work had to be made far more appealing than it ever had been before. The old nine to five was boring. Being an entrepreneur was not.

Even as it was being used to sex up work, the romantic notion of entrepreneurship and individualism was being used to justify major shifts in the way countries were run. In the UK, this meant the sale of public sector companies (gas, electricity, the railways) to private investors. The powerful unions, which represented employees of these companies, saw their power eroded dramatically. This was justified, and probably rightly so, because they were seen as being way too powerful.

* * *

In the early and again in the late '80s, UK advertising was walloped by recession. Agencies constricted rapidly and dramatically. A huge number of people, especially "creatives", had no choice but to become self-employed if they wanted to stay in the business.

People like Eric, Phillip and me who set up small agencies like Mighty Mouse in the late 1980s, were already living the entrepreneurial, individualistic dream. Often, whether we wanted to or not. But, we were pretty sure we were in control of our own destiny – apart from being at the mercy of clients, of course.

This is what's happening today in many countries and industries all over the world. It's the '80s all over again. According to Shane Snow, journalist, geek, and chief commercial officer of Contently, "About a third of journalists and creative workers are already independent and that number is going to rise". Shane says, this is because work is no longer a place (a great way of putting it), and the Internet lets companies find the best person to do anything anywhere.

(While I was writing this book, Ronald Coase, an incredibly important British economist, died. In 1937, in his groundbreaking essay "The Nature of the Firm", Coase asked the question, "Why do companies exist"? His conclusion was because of the "transactional cost" of doing things in-house. Now, although the Internet makes it easier for organisations to outsource to service providers like Shane's and to save costs, firms or companies are actually as important as they were when Coase was writing.

While I am definitely not in favour of a conventional firm, I absolutely agree that organisations, of some form, are far stronger than individuals, and this is key to the third way of working, which we will come to shortly, and which we believe in.

To be successful, freelancers have to think like "de-facto entrepreneurs", as Shane puts it, and, while that's fine for people like Eric and me, it may not be the case for everyone.

Also, you might be what they call a "digital nomad", and have all the freedom in the world, but you still can't build a business that's bigger than one person: you. (2)

However, if you're the kind of person who has the qualities it takes to be self-employed - if you're lucky enough to fit the mould - then you have the qualities needed for the way work is changing in today's world. For better or worse.

* * *

To be successfully self-employed you need discipline, flexibility, resourcefulness and drive. And, in a creative industry, it helps if you have a bit of talent. All of these are fantastic qualities, of course. But there are negative aspects of being self-employed – just as there are in working for a big corporation.

In talking with friends who are self-employed in my industry, freelance creative writers or designers, I learned that they look out for no one other than themselves because they have learned that this is the way to survive – the agencies they work for have no loyalty to them. Agencies use these freelancers if they deliver the goods on time and at a price that allows the agency a very nice mark-up. So my friends charge what they can get away with. They're in a true dog-eat-dog world. However you dress it up, this is capitalism at its rawest.

Many freelancers will happily steal clients away from each other if they can, so they learn to be careful about mentioning the names of their clients. They admit to poaching clients themselves. This is easy for them to square with their consciences because they have no sense of community with their fellow freelancers. It can be a lonely way to work.

This is one price my freelance friends pay for what they believe is a way of working that gives them maximum freedom and allows them to employ themselves. But that does not mean they like it. Would you? Do you?

My freelance friends don't want to be disloyal to people they like and with whom they enjoy working. They don't want to steal business from other people. They want to succeed quite simply because they are very good at what they do. Which is being creative.

It's probably no coincidence that the idea that creative work and being creative about how you work is becoming highly desirable all over again. We all want to be seen as creative, don't we? It's empowering. It's who we are, we think. Today, whether someone is a plumber or a chef, we don't find it strange to say that they take a creative approach to what they do. Creativity has also become about attitude.

Let me tell you what creativity means to me. I believe it's important.

* * *

As a strategic thinker and creative worker, my ability to do my job well depends to a large extent on using what I believe is fundamentally a natural talent. (My mother had been a journalist early on in her career, and my father a book-a-holic; so our house was always full of books, which obviously had something to do with my interests and aspirations.) My work is defined as creative. That is not to say that it can't sometimes be extremely hard work. I am not implying that it is the same as doing open heart surgery, but you know what I mean.

This is important because it's something that people who dream of working at something creative often don't understand. Good, experienced "creatives", as we're called in advertising, learn that we can never kid ourselves. We stand or fall by the quality of our latest work, by our bright ideas. We are the first people to know if an idea is rubbish or not and, believe me, we often wish we didn't. Especially when it's our own work. This is why we keep going, pushing ourselves until we come up with something we can truly stand behind and say: "I know this is great".

Do we just waft around staring into space? Actually, I sometimes do, but generally not when anyone's watching. After all, where do you get your best ideas? Probably not in an office.

Jon Favreau, President Barack Obama's 27-year-old speechwriter, wrote the President's first inauguration speech in a Starbucks and JK Rowling, creator of

Harry Potter, swears by a café as the best place to write. Those of us tapping away in coffee shops are in good company. (3)

In my experience, I'm at my most creative when I am part of a collective effort to crack a brief, to come up with a great idea. When I feel valued and confident that I can really push the boundaries of my own creativity. Key to this has always been having a good and often brave client.

So I know what it's like to do a creative job – and to take a creative approach to employment. I know how hard it is. And, sorry, but I would say you're either creative or you're not. You may wear jeans to work, or spend part of your working day in a coffee shop tapping away at your laptop (like I sometimes do), but that's not being creative. It's just working differently.

This is important because one of the ways governments are responding to the impact of the 2007/2008 worldwide financial crisis is to encourage self-employment. Let's spend a moment and consider this.

Globally there is a dramatic shift taking place in employment norms. We are seeing a large rise in the number of self-employed people around the world. Some observers in the US have called this the rise of the 1099 economy, a term derived from the form Americans fill in and and file to the IRS (US tax authorities) to denote their self employed status in their annual tax assessment. This 1099 economy is predicted to count for a large and growing proportion of the total US working population within the next decade. Although the US self-employment rates are a topic that are debated, some commentators predict that self employed people will account for a major proportion of the US total workforce. In an article on GIGAOM, a US blog that follows technology, Gene Zaino, CEO of MBO Partners, predicts in a report from his company that there will be 65 to 70 million independent workers within the next decade. That's a really big number. The same report also states that the majority of people in independent work chose it, and had not been forced into it, and that a large number of those in traditional employment are considering moving across to work independently because of the lifestyle benefits and because of a lack on fulfilment with traditional employment. It's a view I strongly share.

This rise in the number of freelance workers obviously raises a number of different issues with regards to insurance, healthcare and pensions etc. These issues vary greatly depending on where in the world you are located. As an independent worker in Sweden for example, provided you are paying your personal tax, the governmental systems for health and pensions will cover you. Even in Sweden however many people will still choose to add into these with additional private funding and coverage.

In the US it is different and the individual really has to make sure they are making the necessary provision for their own insurances, healthcare and pensions etc. as well as paying the appropriate taxes to the federal and state government. This is such an important and relevant topic, a number of special support groups and even unions have been established in the US to help self-employed people, or freelancers, manage these tasks.

The main issue here is that the onus is on the individual to manage this important aspect of their lives (it comes down to one of my favourite words – self-responsibility).

One other important topic for freelance consultants to be aware of, again a topic that varies depending on where you live, is the area of single source income. In some countries, as a freelancer or self-employed person, should your source of income or revenue come from a single source or customer, some tax authorities will view this as an employment situation. We stress to all of our members, and indeed believe it's an important factor in developing true independence and security, that having a number of sources of income and "clients" makes a lot of sense. I do the same myself, and have a number of "clients" one of which is UP. It's an important aspect of how the world is changing and that most of us nowadays prefer to spread our work and income over a number of clients, activities and sources. It makes sense and helps you take more control of your life.

* * *

On the plus side, for people who are comfortable with being self-employed or are naturally entrepreneurial, the radical change taking place in ways of working really is an enormous, exciting opportunity, that brings a real upside in the freedom it offers.

We're seeing the emergence of what's being called the 'micro-entrepreneur". These are people who make money in a whole variety of different ways. They use platforms like Ebay or Etsy to generate income by buying and selling. They rent out their spare bedroom via Airbnb. They do the work they like to do as and when they can. They're also part of a sharing economy, which goes some way to meeting the need for community and belonging, something which is very important for me. (4)

This is what is fundamentally different from the 1980s, when we were encouraged to "go it alone". The Internet offers us the potential to be connected, to form communities.

* * *

As you've probably guessed, I'm more than a little ambivalent about what the 80s did for and to me. It provided the context for me to pursue and realise my dream of being self-employed and the CEO of Julian Stubbs Inc. It enabled me to do creative work in an industry that I love.

But, because such a premium was placed on the value of working hard and independently, the 1980s also helped scupper my work-life balance, setting a pattern that helped put me in the position where it took someone like my friend and lifestyle coach Niki Tramontana to give me a wake-up call about my health that was like a cup of cold water in the face at six am in the morning.

And, without making too tenuous a connection, you could view the state of my health as a bit of a metaphor (I am a writer after all) for the price we're paying now, for the more excessive aspects of the '80s ideology.

Continuous consumption. A belief that economic growth is constant and endless and good, and should be fuelled whatever the cost – a disconnect between money and real value. Ignoring the impact we have on our planet and our responsibility to preserve the environment. A conviction that the individual matters more than the community and, beyond that, society. It was all about me, me, me.

I believed that all of these were either good or simply didn't matter. I was wrong. This is why I'm such a fervent believer in the benefits of working in the cloud to build a business that harnesses all of the best aspects of online communities: loyalty, a common goal, a willingness to share and, most of all, trust. But mainly it's about self-responsibility. Because you can't have a strong community without taking responsibility for yourself.

Self-responsibility is the fundamental factor in getting the work-life balance right according to Cali Williams Yost, author of Tweak It: *Make What Matters to You Happen Every Day*. Writing for Fastcompany.com, Cali looks at what she calls "work+life fit naturals" and identifies them as people who realise the following:

"It's their responsibility to make what matters to them happen, day-to-day, in the face of competing demands. They know that no one is going to tell them when to finish a work project, get to the gym, learn new job skills, get their car serviced, or take their son to the movies".

Cali could be describing the members of our online community business.

Self-employment

Interview with Netsize
by David Holzer, UP member

Why Netsize works with UP and an agency based in the cloud.
Netsize, a Gemalto company, is the global leader for mobile operator micro-payment and messaging. The company connects and contracts directly to the carriers and helps their customers monetize mobile services or services linked to mobility, improve brand awareness, acquire new customers, manage customer relationships, and optimize business efficiency, globally. The Netsize payment network reaches more than two billion consumers. Netsize connects more than 1,000 companies to over 160 mobile network operators and provides solutions for distribution channels for vending, ticketing and parking; as well as for services like mobile marketing, hosting and service management. Netsize employs more than 250 telecom professionals and has local offices in 21 countries.

Donya Ekstrand, group marketing communications director for Netsize, explains why the company works with UP THERE, EVERYWHERE.

* * *

Why does Netsize work with UP?

Netsize is a global organisation, and the fact that UP is able to put together teams of really creative people who are from different cultures, actually live in different parts of the world and understand how media are used and really work in these places is really valuable to us. It makes the creative process much more global.

It's great that I can also specify the nationality of team members I'd like to work on my account – writers who write in their native languages, for instance.

Working around the clock is a definite advantage. I love it when work is waiting for me in the morning even though the person who did it is fast asleep.

And I think it's good that all UP members run their own business as part of the organisation. It shows that members are people who are innovative, hardworking and have business savvy. I get quality creative from a business person and I really like that.

> *Working around the clock is a definite advantage. I love it when work is waiting for me in the morning even though the person who did it is fast asleep.*

> *Technology has created a permanent fifth dimension in our lives – virtual space. Every time human beings have perceived a new dimension, it's led to seismic changes in society* (5)

Mark Curtis,
Distraction: Being Human in the Digital Age

Chapter #4

One way or another?

WHERE DO YOU GET YOUR BEST IDEAS?

PROBABLY NOT IN AN OFFICE.

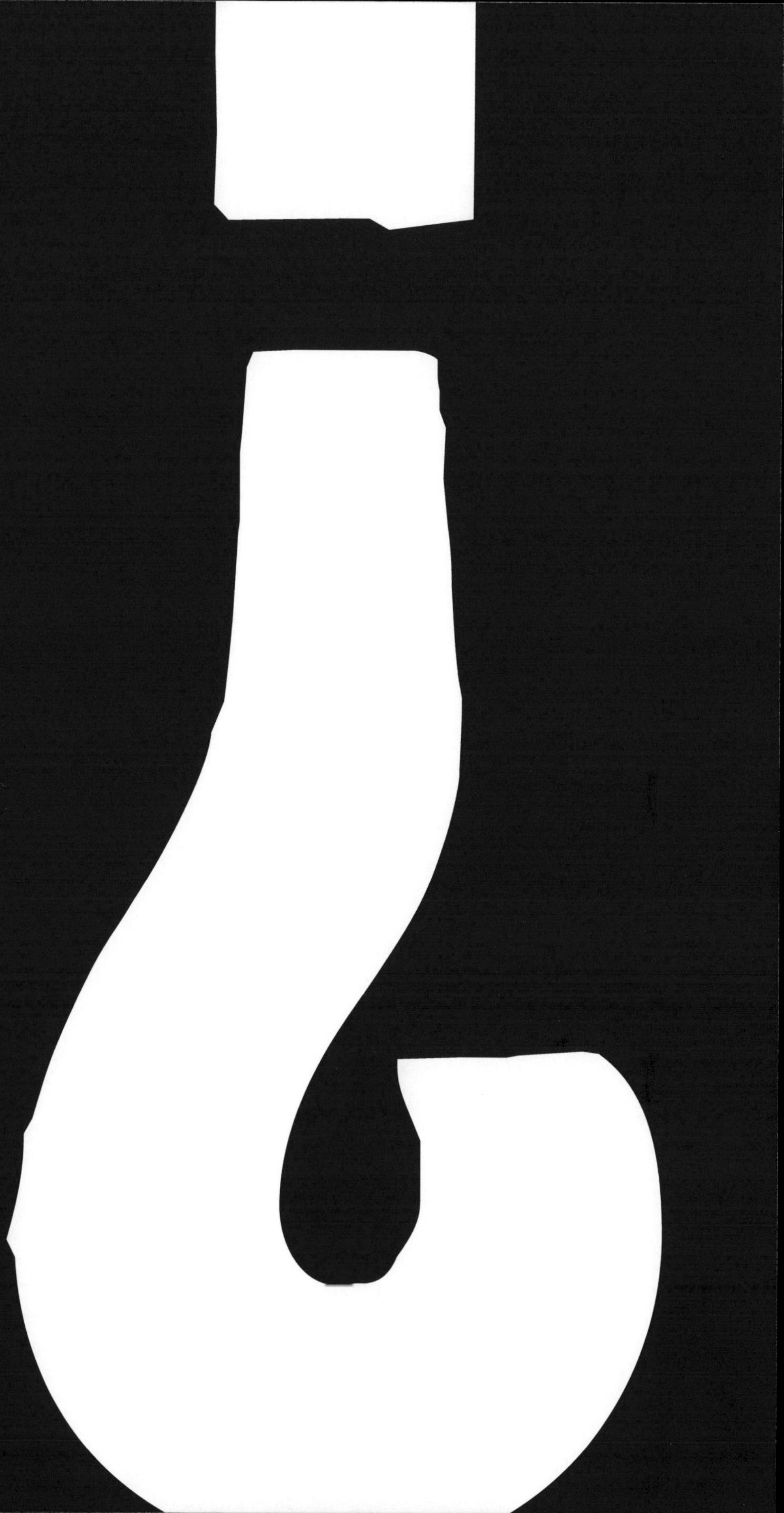

In our brave new world of employment, whether we work online or not, we seem to face two stark choices: from full employment to not working at all, of course). But, before we get to that, let's look at what appear to be our two most realistic options at the moment.

* * *

In late 2012, Marissa Mayer, newly appointed CEO of Yahoo! issued a memo – or rather had Jackie Reses, her head of Public Relations do it – that asked Yahoo! employees who worked remotely to come back to the corporate offices. Disgruntled employees leaked the memo online. What was Mayer's logic?:

"Speed and quality are often sacrificed when we work from home... we need to be one Yahoo!, and that starts with physically being together".

Yahoo! employees affected by this were particularly annoyed because they believed they had been hired with the freedom to work flexibly, as is standard throughout Silicon Valley.

Mayer's memo caused a storm in the media because she seemed to be flying in the face of the standard defenses of remote working: greater productivity, cost-saving, less impact on the environment and, particularly important for women, the opportunity to have a healthier family work-life balance.

As you might expect, commentators from Richard Branson down to yours truly, weighed in with their opinions.

The productivity benefits of remote working are many and the real fear of traditional organisations to adopting it stems normally from a lack of systems to truly measure productivity or more simply a fear of not being in complete control of the employee. (6)

But, despite the advantages, the study also found a downside that related to the way management appeared to view employees. Rates of promotion were reduced by 50% among remote workers. (Although they had roughly the same number of promotions as those who worked on site, they should have had more because they worked harder.) The researchers suggested that this was because remote workers were "out of sight, out of mind" and much less likely to be promoted. The study also found that there was inevitably less interpersonal contact between bosses and other employees, which meant "less opportunity to brainstorm ideas".

When I interviewed *Fortune* business writer Stanley Bing for this book, he said:

"I believe Marissa Mayer of Yahoo! had a point because I don't believe important, dynamic organisations can be made out of people just working remotely".

Other commentators agreed with Stanley and argued that the problem was that Yahoo! had missing employees who nobody knew were still working at the company. Bringing workers together and getting them into the right mindset is obviously a widely recognised corporate approach so, again, it seems that Mayer was thinking on the right lines. (7)

So, really, Mayer's decision was not an attack on remote working itself. It was more of an admission that it wasn't working for Yahoo! because the company hadn't gotten it right.

Responding to a blog post of mine on the subject in early 2013, Peter Bjellerup, an IBM Social Business Consultant, wrote:

"To be able to work remotely, your systems and processes have to support it, as has the culture. Using an extreme analogy: remote working and clocking don't mix well. If you allow employees to work from home, but don't change your systems and processes and maintain a culture of control instead of trust, it simply won't work. Just to take a practical aspect: If your manager cannot see you working (since you work from home) and you don't trust your manager with understanding the value you really bring to your company, you may well end up doing some "self-marketing" to your manager – most commonly in the shape of cc:ing your manager on most mails you send, as a proxy of being productive. "I email, therefore I am". If that is the prevailing culture, your managers will soon end up spending the majority of their time filing cc'd mails instead of doing valuable work. The good response to that is to establish an internal collaborative and social platform. The bad response is to pull everybody back to the office."

As far as I'm concerned, even if remote working (still don't like that phrase) is the way of the future, whenever you work for a corporation you are still not the master of your destiny. And let's not forget that the concept of remote working is not new. In the early days of my career, I worked in a company with a sales force of 1,000 and they didn't feel the need to see each other regularly. Provided sales people met their target they were free to do whatever they wanted. Remote working succeeds when clear goals are set.

I have friends in large corporations who live in fear that they'll be "let go" in the next round of cuts, no matter how good they are at their job or whether they're working remotely or in an office. Thankfully, I've just about forgotten what it must be like to feel like that – to have no control over my destiny, no matter how hard I work, no matter how good I am at my job, no matter how long I've been with a corporation.

So, are you in any better position if you're a freelancer or starting a conventional small business?

***

As I've said, you have to be the right type of individual to succeed as a small business person or self-employed person, to be able to cope with the insecurity, loneliness and competition coming from equally hungry businesses undercutting you all the time. But, if you are, what does the landscape look like to you?

* * *

We're being told, Americans especially, that our future as workers depends on our ability and willingness to become small business owners and self-employed people. The big difference this time around is the way remote working and teleworking from home can be part of the equation.

In America, in particular, small business has traditionally been seen as an engine for growth. But, today, that doesn't seem to be the case, certainly not in the US anyway.

* * *

A "McKinsey Quarterly Chart Focus" newsletter says "Small businesses, defined as companies with fewer than 500 employees, account for almost two-thirds of all net new job creation. They also contribute disproportionately to innovation, generating 13 times as many patents, per employee, as large companies do.

Sadly, small-business optimism is at its lowest levels in almost 20 years. After crashing in the recession, confidence remains below any level recorded since the early 1990s, because the recovery has been so anemic. Had small business come out of the recession maintaining just the rate of start-ups generated in 2007, the US economy would today have almost 2.5 million more jobs than it does."

So, although small business and self-employment are being pushed as the way of the future, perhaps people should remember the fall-out from the 1980s, back in the '90s when it got very tough to be in business for yourself.

But what if you could be in business for yourself, and could draw on a community of like-minded individuals to offer support and share your vision?

Like I said, there's a third way.

* * *

However, we choose to work (if given the choice), the technology is here to stay. While researching this book, I came across the work of Mark Curtis, author of *Distraction: Being Human in the Digital Age*. Curtis says "Technology has created a permanent fifth dimension in our lives – virtual space. Every time human beings have perceived a new dimension, it's led to seismic changes in society. We moved from thinking in two dimensions in Medieval art to three dimensions in the Renaissance. In Dante, Heaven and Hell were in a direct line up and down. At the same time Copernicus and Galileo started to realize there was something called space, which completely undermined the whole notion of Heaven, because if space is infinite then where is Heaven? That fundamentally changed the way we see everything".

We are incredibly fortunate that we can use that "permanent fifth dimension".

* * *

UP member David Holzer, who lives in Mallorca, Spain, was on a trip to Morocco in spring 2013, staying at the Hotel Continental in Tangier. Every night, as the sun went down, the city squares filled with young, able-bodied men looking out to sea and dreaming of making it the seven miles across the Straits of Gibraltar to Spain and a chance of work.

We should never forget that although we're privileged enough to explore the fifth dimension, we also live in a real world.

Interview with Kate Adams
by David Holzer, UP member

A collective of minds: An interview with Kate Adams, Managing Director of UP North America, Kate has led client engagements for global brands like Forbes Media, GE Life Sciences, Time Warner Cable Business Class and T Mobile. Kate, who is British, is based at the UP New York Creative Space in SoHo. We were all delighted when Kate joined UP, bringing with her a strong blend of traditional client services expertise and a naturally forward-looking perspective. I described her as a "digital native" and she politely put me straight. Today, the term is an oxymoron.

What do you think are the differences between UP and a more conventional agency?
Our real core strength, and it can only get stronger, is our ability to create expansive ideas contributed by an incredible collection of minds from all over the world. A collective of minds hand-picked for the client's need and challenge.

How does that work in practice?
Like a traditional agency, we put teams onto client accounts and grow business organically. This provides clients with consistency and the confidence that the agency team is learning, knows the brand and can provide the advice and expertise you'd expect from a strategic and creative partner.

The difference is that traditional agencies are also required to make sure employees are working to full capacity and being profitable. This means that the people on an account are not necessarily those most suitable or qualified. It's here where the UP model gives us a huge advantage over traditional agencies, which I feel are almost institutions. We can walk into any room and honestly tell a client, "Yes, this is your team". Why? Because we can pick the most expert and best equipped individual to work on an account. And it's in the team's interest to do so. Our cloud-based model and the idea of e-ployment make this possible.

How do you think advertising itself is changing?
From my perspective, it's changing rapidly and aggressively, and the agency institutions are failing to keep up. They simply can't move quickly enough. It would also be too expensive and time-consuming to change, as this would mean altering the very core of their infrastructure. So they outsource more and more, as we're seeing. But working extensively with specialist freelancers is hardly viable when it comes to building the expertise and consistency of knowledge that brands demand. I think agencies are petrified. Of agencies like UP, of individuals, and of how they are going to keep their investors happy.

The industry needs more agencies like UP if it is truly going to deliver great creative ideas.
Young talent coming through was educated and raised with the belief that nothing is out of reach for them as individuals, which makes them bigger thinkers and fiercely independent. They don't want to be institutionalised in agencies or constrained by the traditional model. In fact, it stifles their creativity. They need to be in a situation they feel in control of.

And, don't forget, these are the minds that are creating the future of communications. Putting the power back in their hands (whether they are artists, strategists, entrepreneurs or writers) to work with the freedom to think creatively without boundaries just makes sense.

I think that as an industry we are at the dawn of some of the best creative thinking and most brilliant ways to communicate with people we have ever seen. And it's coming from young talent working closely with and being guided by very smart, independent (and in many cases) more senior minds who themselves get a kick out of working without boundaries. UP is helping young talent expand and do amazing things while offering the structure a traditional agency would provide. Giving them the best of both worlds.

Why is UP right for North America now?
Being an ex-pat I have a slightly different view of the place than many natives perhaps do. When it comes to our industry, there is really no place like it (in size, talent, diversity of people, or technology and innovation). It sounds corny, but you really can make things happen here (cue Frank Sinatra!) People gravitate to and celebrate the next big thing, the innovators who are spurring change. This, after all, is how America became "America". Team that up with European smarts, product research and development, and a different world view (perhaps a more balanced one), and you have an amazing offering.

One that is truly global, challenges the status quo, is constantly in tune with "glocal" changes, influences and happenings and is driven by the desire of individuals who are already successful to work with a team of like minds and achieve great things.

The men of Madison Avenue created the industry, but we're about to reinvent it. UP and the concept of e-ployment are providing the platform to allow us to do it now, quickly and on a grand scale.

I'm excited to be at the forefront of this radical reinvention and, through UP, to help make it happen. UP is the game changer right now. We, our clients and our members have a head start.

> *(We can) access learning, retrain, engage in commerce, seek or advertise a job, invent, invest and crowd source – all online. But this huge expansion in an individual's ability to do all these things comes with one big difference: more now rests on you*

Thomas Friedman,
The World is Flat

Chapter #5
Dog feed dog

a whole new

flattened world

In this chapter I'm going to refer to astrology, evolution and one of the pioneers of communism. Why, you might ask? (And as an aside, I'd like to state I'm very much apolitical, not right or left wing and if anything have totally lost faith in most politicians and political parties. But I guess that just makes me like the majority of people these days.)

***

When Eric and I started kicking around the idea for an online community business, it didn't take long for us to realise that if the idea of working this way appealed to us there was no reason why it wouldn't catch on with people like us. It seemed like the time was right.

Here's where astrology and evolution come in.

***

In the immortal words of Jim Morrison of the Doors, "I don't believe in astrology". But for some reason that I can't remember, I was having a conversation with a friend who does and she mentioned that we're in the Age of Aquarius (which co-incidentially is my star sign). All I could think of was the song from the hippie musical Hair, but the friend went on to say that the Age of Aquarius gave us the Internet.

"Why"? I asked, intrigued.

"Well", she said, "Aquarius emphasises groups and communities, which is why we have the Internet and television. It's a very social sign. But Aquarius is really all about communities of leaders".

Which is exactly what we are creating: a community of leaders.

So what about evolution?

***

I'm extremely grateful to Simon Cohen, broadcaster, public speaker, moral and social commentator and all-around nice guy for introducing me to the work of Kropotkin and pointing out its relevance for a new way of doing business.

Wikipedia describes Prince Pyotr Alexeyevich Kropotkin (1842-1921) as a "Russian zoologist, evolutionary theorist, philosopher, scientist, revolutionary, philologist, economist, activist, geographer, writer and prominent anarcho-communist". A man of many facets, let's just say. Now I'm not exactly a communist (as I stated earlier pretty much apolitical) but his ideas are worth reflecting on. Kropotkin wanted a communist society "free from central government and based on voluntary associations between workers". The key word here is voluntary.

In 1902, Kropotkin published *Mutual Aid: A Factor of Evolution*, which offered an alternative view of evolution to that put forward by "social Darwinists," who argued that it was all about survival of the fittest, the dog-eat-dog philosophy that drove capitalism from the late nineteenth century onward, and which has arguably led us as a society to where we are today.

Kropotkin argued "that it was evolutionary emphasis on cooperation instead of competition in the Darwinian sense that made for the success of species, including the human". (9)

In the last chapter of *Mutual Aid,* Kropotkin wrote:

"The animal species, in which individual struggle has been reduced to its narrowest limits, and the practice of mutual aid has attained the greatest development, are invariably the most numerous, the most prosperous, and the most open to further progress. The mutual protection which is obtained in this case, the possibility of attaining old age and of accumulating experience, the higher intellectual development, and the further growth of sociable habits, secure the maintenance of the species, its extension, and its further progressive evolution. The unsociable species, on the contrary, are doomed to decay."

Eric's and my belief in mutual aid and protection is one of the founding principles of UP. I favor this over the isolated life of the freelancer or the drone in the conventional company any day of the week, wouldn't you?

The third influence on UP, apart from our personal situation, was the work of Thomas Freidman. But before we get into Friedman, we need to set the scene a little.

★ ★ ★

In 1983, a cover article in Time magazine referred to "The New Economy". This term described the transition from heavy industry to a new technology-based economy that was one of the factors that helped shape the 1980s. But it wasn't until the late 1990s, when the US economy (and the economies of countries whose fortunes were most linked to it) really began to grow, that the term caught on. Some economists attribute this growth to the computer truly coming of age with the Internet and, specifically, the cloud. For instance, in his book, *The Big Switch: Rewiring the World, from Edison to Google*, Nicholas Carr makes a convincing case when he states that the impact of the cloud on business and society is as momentous as electricity becoming widely available at the end of the nineteenth century.

Before the Internet and, later, the cloud, a computer was just a box in a room.

The term "The New Economy" was taken up by politicians and thinkers of all persuasions and applied to a new era in which new technologies became integrated into the international economy at the same time as corporations were restructuring and laying people off. One of the outcomes was that individuals were forced to become flexible, rootless entrepreneurs. (10)

"The New Economy" clearly helped pave the way for globalisation; and in my mind, Friedman is the great commentator on what "The New Economy" and globalisation means for people and employment. People like us, who are looking for a new way of working.

* * *

Thomas Friedman's 2005 treatise, *The World Is Flat: A Brief History of the Twenty-First Century* presents his take on globalisation. It came about when he was on assignment in India to work on a documentary about outsourcing for the Discovery Channel, and he was shocked to find out just how many things could actually be outsourced. I read the book three years after it first came out and it had an immediate and profound impact on my view of what was happening.

The title of the book is a metaphor for seeing the world as a level playing field, in which commerce and all competitors have equal opportunities. It makes an important point for me personally - in my work as a brand strategist - in that cities, countries, companies and individuals need to shift gears mentally, to remain competitive in a truly global market where historical and geographical divisions are becoming ever more irrelevant. And Friedman makes the point that this Globalization 3.0 is driven by a convergence of personal computers, broadband fibre optics and what he calls workflow software, increasingly powered by the cloud.

I won't go into *The World Is Flat* in any degree of detail, but I recommend that you read it. What resonated most strikingly with me relates to what he says about globalisation and the fortunes of individuals.

Friedman argues that globalised "individuals have to think globally to thrive, or at least survive" and to be successful takes "technological expertise, mental flexibility, self-motivation and psychological mobility".

For the individuals who can adapt to the new flat world, there will be plenty of jobs for people willing to work hard. We just have to let go of the idea of lifetime employment and replace it with "lifetime employability".

I absolutely agree with him, and this is one of the drivers behind the business Eric, I and a growing number of like minds are building. For me, and most of the people in our community, it's about being able to do the work you love for as long as you can. We want to be able to work for life.

(Friedman's perspectives have also influenced my thinking on an area close to my own heart, cities and destinations. Global competition doesn't just affect corporations and individuals; cities and destinations have to change the way they think and act. In my speeches, I always like to remind people that: "As one place markets itself, every other place has to".)

In *The World is Flat*, talking about what he calls "The New Middlers", that is, "former middle-class workers who can upgrade their skills to become effective managers of people or information. (11) Friedman develops the idea of becoming an "untouchable" when it comes to employment.

Untouchables are people "whose jobs cannot be outsourced, digitised or automated". They are:

Great Collaborators and Orchestrators

The Great Synthesisers

The Great Explainers

The Great Leveragers

The Great Adaptors

The Passionate Personalisers

The Great Localisers.

Untouchables manage people and information. They explain complexity. They're versatile in adapting to new technology. They have expertise in "green technology". They can adapt enterprise-level practices to small business.

I am proud to be an untouchable.

A couple of other things Friedman mentions are also relevant for the concept of UP. He writes about the concept of trust: "Trust is the most important factor in any relationship, particularly cross cultural relationships and culture provides the framework for how well we work together, and how well we treat strangers". (12)

This really resonates with what we are doing at UP. Within the enterprise we were building, Eric and I wanted to extend the bond of trust that had grown up between us over all the years we had worked together. We reached out to people we trusted first. They then reached out to people they trusted. This started with Lawrence in Amsterdam, a truly gifted business developer and "people person" - a natural to head up our own people recruitment operation. Then there was Peter, in Malmö, southern Sweden, one of the most talented designers and typographers I have ever met (and designer of this book). Then Bill in London, a senior creative we had known for years. Shari, a digital and social media queen based at the heart of it, in Boston. Very quickly in these early days a strong, and global, team was naturally taking shape.

Friedman also argues that one way for small companies to flourish in the flat world is by learning to act really big. The key to this is taking advantage of new collaboration tools to reach "further, faster, wider and deeper". (13)

Eric and I saw our community business as a natural evolution of our use of technologies like iChat, Facetime, Skype and Dropbox to communicate, and they are one of the reasons we're able to grow and flourish.

***

While Thomas Friedman's thinking has had an unquestionable influence on my own, I don't entirely agree with him when he argues that it's up to the individual to look after themselves.

I agree with Friedman that more now rests on us, but - and this is where the Age of Aquarius and Kropotkin come in - I would argue that it's also precisely why we need online communities that offer us real mutual aid when it comes to employment.

And, I would also argue that companies that are looking for individuals who can deliver the skills they need, but behind a brand they can trust and within a framework they can rely on, can also benefit from working with an online community.

Mutual aid and trust also drive the relationship between clients and suppliers. If we don't have mutual aid and trust, we return to the hyper-manic dog-eat-dog days of the 1980s, which I and many of my fellow community members lived through. We were able to flourish in such a competitive business environment, and it taught us a lot. But, as I said earlier in this book, we also regret how short-sighted it made us, having to focus on the ferocious competition.

Now, before we go into more detail of how Eric and I got our community off the ground, let's consider how online communities evolved along with the Internet. This will give us a better idea of the strategic thinking behind what we're creating, which needs to be applied to any online community business.

Interview

with Dag Ulrik Kühle-Gotovac, Nobel Institute
by David Holzer, UP member

In March 2011, the Nobel Peace Prize Concert Company and International Management Group (IMG), the organisation that plans the Nobel Peace Prize Concert, asked UP to create a fresh identity, website and social media program for the Concert. Nobel felt that what existed didn't reflect the contemporary nature of the concert.

A key element for Nobel was that the project team needed to be truly international with members in Sweden, Norway and the US able to work with client teams in those locations.

This was the very early days of UP and we were obviously thrilled to have landed such a fantastic project.

We designed a fresh new graphic identity, an exciting and interactive website and developed a Facebook page and YouTube channel to help grow the audience for the event. We also created a national advertising campaign that ran in Norway, as well as the Nobel Peace Prize Concert's first online advertising, which included Facebook, Twitter, YouTube and banner ads.

Since 2011, UP has continued to work with IMG and the Nobel Peace Prize Concert to update the website each year and manage a social media and advertising campaign for the Concert.

I caught up with Dag Ulrik Kühle-Gotovac, head of administration for the Nobel Institute. I started by asking him what convinced Nobel to choose an unknown agency with a radical new business model.

Why did Nobel invite UP to pitch for the initial work?

One of our main contacts at IMG met Julian when he was giving a speech a few years back. The way he spoke about the Nobel brand and the Nobel Peace Prize in particular made us want to talk to him when the time came to improve the Nobel Peace Prize Concert identity.

Funnily enough, people are a little scared of Nobel, so we don't usually get approached. We actually have to go out and find what we need, which is great because it means we're in the driver's seat.

To be honest, the director of the Institute was very sceptical. He's used to things like this costing a lot of money and taking a long time. We were all delighted with UP's work but he, in particular, was convinced by Julian and satisfied with the end result. Not to mention the speed at which everything was delivered.

Was the way UP works (being cloud-based with no offices) a factor in your decision?

Not initially. All we require from our partnerships is that people are attentive to our needs; where this comes from is not especially important. But I must say that I quickly learned to appreciate the fact that UP works in different time zones globally. Working around the clock meant that things happened very fast, and I liked the fact that I could send a question to UP and get an answer within my working day or in the evening.

What do you think is UP's main strength?

The big picture, I'd say. You're strong in your main purpose and deliver on time. The people have a good energy, which means working with you feels great. This might be because UP members love what they're doing and have an appropriate work-life balance.

Your relationship with UP is ongoing, could you tell me why?

We have a tradition in all areas of work of picking people we trust and sticking with them as long as the relationship is mutually beneficial. This makes it possible for us to keep the level of knowledge about what we do high throughout our extended organisation and helps us keep our inner circle lean.

What do you think UP's way of working could offer Norway?

Even though Norwegians, like people in so many other countries, are slowly converging on urban areas, the Norwegian government is still focused on helping people stay put and develop their communities. I can see that working online and having flexibility will mean that people with certain skill sets and the inclination to stay local will be able to remain in their communities and continue to be healthy and prosperous.

> *Big Brother is Watching You*
>
> George Orwell
> 1984

Chapter #6

1984 and beyond

HUMAN CONNECTION ON A VAST SCALE HUMAN CONNECTION ON A VAST SCALE HUMAN CONNECTION ON A VAST SCALE HUMAN CONNECTION ON A VAST SCALE HUMAN CONNECTION ON A VAST SCALE HUMAN CONNECTION ON A VAST SCALE HUMAN CONNECTION ON A VAST SCALE HUMAN CONNECTION ON A VAST SCALE HUMAN CONNECTION ON A VAST SCALE HUMAN CONNECTION ON A VAST SCALE HUMAN CONNECTION ON A VAST SCALE HUMAN CONNECTION ON A VAST SCALE HUMAN CONNECTION ON A VAST SCALE HUMAN CONNECTION ON A VAST SCALE

HUMAN CONNECTION ON A VAST SCALE

Winston Smith and George Orwell's 1984 have played a big part in my life. Reading the book for the first time as a kid didn't just give me a glimpse of the future. It was a warning of the potential intrusiveness of authority. The book was first published in 1948 (Orwell reversed the date to get 1984), and it made some prescient predictions about the future of society. For instance, television that can watch you as well as broadcast at the same time is now a part of our lives.

While I was writing this book, it was revealed that the US National Security Agency (NSA) had been rooting around in data stored in the cloud. I can't say that this worries me, but it's clearly the case that online media offers any government enormous opportunity to snoop.

So, how did we arrive at today's totally "networked" and connected society?

* * *

Did you know that the word "Internet" comes from "internetworking"? It's fitting, given that this book is all about the future of working online in extended communities of networks. The word first appeared in December 1974, in a document called the "Internet Transmission Control Program".

By 1973, even before the Internet got its name, email was the most popular tool associated with the fledgling "net". Believe it or not, online chatting also came about in the early 1970s. So social networking is nothing new. It has a history and a context, as does online community business, and it's this that I want to look at.

* * *

I am what's known as a digital citizen rather than a digital native – the latter being someone like my son who has grown up with the technology – which means that I can remember a time before the Internet became ubiquitous. The Internet actually dates as far back as the early 1960s, when the first packet switching technology was introduced by the US Advanced Research Projects Agency Network (ARPANET). Widely regarded as the backbone of the modern Internet, ARPANET was created by the US Department of Defense to use in projects at universities and research labs.

In 1969, the first four sites were connected; email came about in 1972. At its beginning you could only send email from one person to another.

The first message group and mailing list appeared in 1975 and the first bulletin board system in 1978. In 1979, Usenet Free software allowed people to share bulletin board discussions.

Fast forward to 1984, and Delphi and Prodigy, the earliest commercial information services pop up. Ironic, when you think of 1984 and Big Brother. America Online, or AOL, was founded in 1985 and offered email. The first commercial Internet Service Providers (ISPs) appeared in the late 1980s. Enter a British computer scientist by the name of Tim Berners Lee who was working at CERN, the European Organization for Nuclear Research, home to the world's largest particle physics laboratory located in Switzerland. Berners Lee had a problem sharing information, so he submitted a proposal for an information management system in March 1989, and then implemented the first successful communication between a Hypertext Transfer Protocol (HTTP) client and server via the Internet sometime around mid-November of that year. On August 6, 1991, the first website was launched at CERN, on the French side running on a NeXT computer (thanks again, Steve Jobs). The site focused on information regarding the new WWW Project – and we've never looked back.

In 1992, AOL connected to the Internet, and in 1994 Netscape introduced the very first graphical web browser.

By 1994, there were an estimated 3.8 million subscribers to commercial online services in the US alone. The history of the Internet is really about human connection on a vast scale. (14)

* * *

My own personal involvement with computers and the Internet is probably fairly typical for people of my generation in business.

In the late 80s, I started my first job in a typical corporate setting. The computer was a huge grey whirring thing in its own room and was connected to a Visual Display Unit (VDU) with a green blinking light on my desk into which I typed orders. The head of computing and his assistant were two of the most important people in the company, because if the computer went down the company was in big trouble. These guys swaggered about the office and drove seriously expensive cars.

The computer didn't impress me much, and I certainly didn't think it would become a major part of my life.

Jump to the early 1990s and I'm working for an agency in Sweden. I encounter my very first Apple Mac. I type stuff into it and play games. It's quite useful and comes with a bag so I can take it home with me and work from there if I want to. Unlike the previous computer thing, this one is user friendly and useful. Very quickly I'm hooked on Apple.

One of the guys in the office tells me I can send things over the company Ethernet to our central office. I think this is really clever. It takes one and a half hours to send a text file, and when it's sent I have to ring up to make sure it arrived.

In 1993 I took a job on the client side and, luckily, the company was using Apple computers. One morning, a colleague breezed into my office, looked at my in and out trays and said, "Oh, you're still on snail mail".

"Excuse me"? I said.

"You've got an email address, you know", he said over his shoulder as he wafted out of my office.

"What's an email address"? I asked my secretary. It turned out we'd had email for a month and the guy was an early adopter.

A little while later the same guy said, "Have you searched yourself"?

I thought about saying "For what"?, but instead I said, "Of course I have". Once again, I had no idea what he meant.

I went to Netscape and typed in my name and, amazingly I got a few hits. I was thrilled. I was up there online. I was really important now.

In the mid-1990s, the company I was working for bought a company in San Francisco and I was appointed head of branding. I went there to get to know my new US counterparts and invited the Head of Sales out to dinner. "I've got a hot tip for you", he said. "Buy shares in a little start-up out of Seattle. It'll make you rich". The little start-up was called Amazon. I'd never heard of it and I didn't buy shares.

* * *

While sniffing around online, I came across a fascinating interview on a blog called Thought Economics (tagline: Interviews with the world's leading thinkers). The interviewer is Vikas Shah, and the interview and thinker is Dr. Vint Cerf, semi-legendary as vice president and chief Internet evangelist for Google, and regarded as one of the fathers of the Internet. Vikas's interview is particularly relevant for the history of online communities it imparts.

Early on in the interview, Vikas quotes Nicholas Carr's 2011 book *The Shallows: What the Internet is Doing to Our Brains.* Talking about what he calls "intellectual technologies", Carr says, "these are our most important tools... for cultivating relations with others".

Carr goes on to point out that the mass communication technologies have unified with the Internet, which in 2011 linked over 30% of the world's population, to such an extent that it's incorporating all other intellectual technologies. This, of course, has accelerated recently with the continuing rise of the mobile Internet.

Cerf begins by answering the question "Why did the Internet grow so quickly"? He explains that it came about: ...at a time when workstations were becoming increasingly popular. There were also no intellectual property restrictions on TCP/IP protocols and these gained credibility... because they worked".

Routers were commercialised in about 1986 by Cisco Systems and others, and networking services became commercially accessible in the US around 1989. "That unleashed a substantial demand because people were very interested in using computers for all kinds of things", according to Cerf. (Like building communities.)

In 1991, Tim Berners Lee launched his World Wide Web (WWW) design, which made the Internet even more useful, and this became commercially available as Netscape in 1994. When that company went public it triggered the infamous dot-com boom and dot-com bust. Despite the dot-com bust, the Internet continued to grow rapidly.

Cerf points out that, unlike most mass media mechanisms such as broadcast television or publishing, the Internet is interactive. Which makes it uniquely perfect for two-way and group communication.

For me, the most telling thing Cerf says is that "the Internet is the first technology we have created that makes us more human". In a subsequent chapter I'll discuss what I think being "human" is in relation to working online as part of a community, but I believe that Cerf is absolutely right.

So now that we have an idea of how the Internet developed, we can move on to the rise and rise of online communities. But before that, let's scan a timeline for cloud computing, without which UP could not exist.

The following timeline derives from Richard Wilberforce's post *"The Growth of The Cloud Computing Industry"* on blog.marketresearch.com:

1961 - John McCarthy, in a speech delivered during MIT's Centennial, states, "computation may someday be organized as a public utility". This became the underlying theory for cloud computing.
1997 - The term cloud computing was officially used for the first time during a lecture by Professor Ramnath K. Challappa, PhD .
1999 - Salesforce.com made its debut as a company delivering enterprise applications through a website.
2002 - Amazon Web Services entered the market by providing storage options, computation, and other web services.
2005 - Eze Castle Industries deploys the first ever hosted cloud platform at a large hedge fund.

2006 - Google announces their entry with the debut of Google Docs. The power of document sharing through the cloud was given to end users.

2006 - Amazon focuses on small businesses and individuals with the introduction of their Elastic Compute cloud (EC2) as a commercial web service.

2009 - Google Apps is released and browser-based enterprise applications through services are set loose on the world.

2009 - Microsoft joins the party with Windows Azure. By providing platform as a service (PaaS) and infrastructure as a service (IaaS), Microsoft aimed to provide a platform for deployment through a global network of Microsoft managed datacenters.

2010 - Salesforce.com releases Database.com and allows for computing services to be used on any platform and in any programming language.

Richard concludes by saying: "In a relatively short amount of time, the cloud has made gigantic strides in the technology landscape. All signs seem to point up, and we are only scratching the surface on cloud computing's true capabilities".

Absolutely, Richard.

* * *

The first online communities developed in the 1970s and were made up of researchers. (Incidentally, experts agree that the first emoticon was a smiley made like so:-). It was invented by Kevin Mackenzie in 1979 to soften the impact of an electronic communication. So we have a Kevin to blame.

The Whole Earth Lectronic Link (WELL.com), which went online in 1985, is regarded as the first non-technical online community. WELL.com is still going strong more than 25 years later and is where a guy called Howard Rheingold came up with term "virtual community". It grew out of the *Whole Earth Review: Tools and Ideas for the Computer Age*, a magazine that built on the incredible success of The Whole Earth Catalog and reviewed the technology from a decidedly countercultural or alternative perspective, and started life as a place where writers and readers of the magazine could get bound up in fierce debate. WELL inspired the great magazine WIRED, possibly the first magazine to make the potential that comes from the application of technology fascinating to non-techies like me.

* * *

Incidentally, the guy behind The Whole Earth, Stewart Brand, is an extraordinary character. He came out of the 1960s American counterculture, broadly defined as being counter to the culture, technology and social structures driving what was regarded as a cold war state. (15) This movement which arguably found its focus on the Berkeley campus of the University of California and went on to influence much of the thinking about computers and the Internet as a space for personal freedom or, as Stewart Brand and his friends called it, the "electronic frontier".

Brand was a huge influence on Steve Jobs, founder of Apple and a hero of mine. In the Stanford commencement address he gave in 2005, Jobs called Brand's The Whole Earth Catalog "one of the bibles of my generation". He goes on to say that the farewell message of The Whole Earth Catalog – "Stay Hungry, Stay Foolish" - is what he's always wished for himself. Me too, kind of.

In a way, what we're doing with UP is in line with Stewart Brand's vision. Not just because it's an online community but also because I agree with him when he simply argues that you can't change human nature. (16)

I'm not much of a lover of the word "management". For me 'management' is a non-productive, bureaucratic function that too often adds little value.

Management generally involves not just management of processes (which should be automated as much as possible anyway) it also involves management of people. That's the worst part. I believe people are at their best when taking full self-responsibility - when they manage themselves within a framework, with clearly defined objectives. Spending time managing people is my least favourite, time-consuming, task. I remember clearly working for one of the most inspiring managers I ever had the pleasure of working with, and on my first day in the office we had a meeting. We sat down and he asked me if I knew my objectives. I said I did. He then asked if I needed a job description. I said absolutely not. Fine, he said, then get on with it. That's my kind of management. If you don't know what you're supposed to do, you are probably the wrong person for the job.

I believe in creating natural systems that help guide people and their actions. The Japanese call this "Poka Yoke" and it basically means mistake proofing, helping an equipment operator avoid (yokeru) mistakes (poka). Isn't "Poka Yoke" great?

Instead of the concept of management, I believe we should think of water flowing down a hill, naturally finding the path of least resistance. We should build systems that help people use the way we're built to work quickly, easily and smoothly.

For its members, our online community business builds on the unchanging soft-wired human need to be part of a community and uses technology to enable this. For clients, it's about changing the way business is done. It's not the dawn of a new civilization, but it's a start!

The invention of the World Wide Web, which sat on top of the Internet and made it far more accessible, made websites much easier to create and put this technology – along with others – in the hands of community organisations.

Additional technologies that fuelled the growth of online communities include the MP3 music file, developed by a German company called Fraunhofer and launched in 1995. For good or bad, this led directly to the formation of file-sharing communities like Napster or Pirate Bay. Open source technology has also led to communities that have come into existence purely because of a single technology.

Today, it's hard to find anyone in some form of employment who isn't on Facebook or LinkedIn, not to mention any number of smaller online communities. At least two-thirds of the online world is on Facebook. These online networks are a fact of life for most of us. I actually have to limit the number of communities I'm part of to not more than 20.

What makes one online community succeessful when others are not? In my opinion, a community is only as effective as its members. This is something we've been sure to bear in mind with UP.

And the immediate future of online communities? When interviewed on blog.leadernetworks.com, Vanessa DiMauro, CEO of Leader Networks, a leader in creating social strategies and online communities for B2B businesses said:

"The future of community is definitely an exciting topic and one that has been a long time in the making. As online communities have only recently become popular, many people don't realize that they have been around and thriving for more than 35 years! Primarily used to support virtual knowledge sharing in professional settings (academics, IT executives, research), they have a proven strength in supporting information exchange and collaboration. So, I believe the history of community will continue to influence their future. The biggest trend I see on the horizon for online communities is the advent of specialized private online communities. In my view, the specialized online community's day has come"! (17)

Couldn't agree more, Vanessa.

But the thing is this. Most of today's online communities are mostly just that – online, living only in the digital fifth dimension.

Apart from hoping that I stay hungry and foolish for the rest of my life, I'm inspired by Stewart Brand and the original pioneers of the electronic frontier who saw the first virtual communities as feeding back into the real world, in my case the very real, very human, offline world of people working together.

Our new electronic frontier is in the world of work, empowering people to support themselves in their own real lives and to create a new work-life balance. Employment now needs to enter the twenty-first century.

Cloud vs Crowd

I want to make an important distinction between the community we're creating and sites that offer work via crowd sourcing. People sometimes ask me if we're a crowd sourcing service, and I point out the critical difference.

Crowd sourcing is a bit like outsourcing to me, finding some way to simply get the lowest cost for delivering a function. As we all know outsourcing takes little account of the communities it impacts or the potential damage it can do to a brand. Let me give you an example.

My mother, who is British, called her well-known UK bank. After three or four rings the call was answered by a very pleasant but obviously foreign lady who was not actually in the UK. After a brief conversation in which my mother struggled to make herself or her request understood (mainly because of the lack of true cultural reference), she hung up – disappointed. Her supposedly UK bank wasn't. It had outsourced.

So, my mother moved her account. She was British and wanted a British bank that was actually British. I use this example purely to demonstrate a point. Outsourcing can damage communities and brands.

In some respects, I equate crowd sourcing in our business as just another way of driving down costs with little added value for the people involved in the process. It doesn't build strong, consistent teams that work on a project as genuine value-adding members.

Don't get me wrong, crowd sourcing does have its place in industries like publishing or film, but in marketing communications it's just another form of third world exploitation. And, if the advantage for "crowdworkers", wherever they are, is that it's a way of making money, it's debatable whether that's even true.

Interview with Rob England
by David Holzer, UP member

Rob England is an ex-client and most importantly a friend. He was also an early member of UP, when I started it with Eric Dowell. Rob started out as a scientist hoping to change the world through agricultural chemistry, specifically improving food production. He pursued this until he was 25 and doing post-PhD work in Sweden related to improving productivity in plants. Rob's personal eureka moment came when he realised that he was more interested in communicating the value of brilliant ideas and making sure they made as much of a difference as possible in the world outside the scientific community.

This led him into marketing communications for life sciences, and today Rob leads UP FOR LIFE, communicating the value of discoveries like groundbreaking new drugs and improvements in cancer diagnostics to end-users.

* * *

What did you know about the cloud before you started working in it?
I thought it was a hype or ploy. I didn't think the cloud could dramatically change ways of doing business. When I started working with things like file sharing and project management involving several parties, I got the point of the cloud. But it was when I became a member of a cloud-based community and started working with other people that I really began to see the benefits.

What were your preconceptions (if any), and have they been reinforced or shattered?
For a start, I wasn't comfortable talking to a computer and not being able to read people through body language and eye contact. These were the ways I decided I could trust people, as we all do. Trust is vital to any collaboration. I learnt by watching my children – seeing my son use Skype at the same time as gaming online, strategizing and talking with other gamers. He was building bonds of trust through non-verbal communication.

Professionally, I believed there was no way you could get a creative team to come up with the same results as they would if they were all in one room. I was wrong.

How do you think an online community business builds trust between its members and with clients?
People have to be nominated by several people to join UP. This method of recruitment is essentially replacing the need to look someone in the eye and decide if they look like a trustworthy person. Now I know great projects can be done by individuals teaming up in the cloud.

How did you end up becoming part of UP?
I trust Julian and Eric.

What is it about UP that appealed/appeals to you?
I get a kick out of my job and I love giving a client a great solution. UP allows me to be even more resourceful when it comes to doing that. I have access to premium talent available from anywhere, and I connect that talent to the job that needs it.

What do you see the advantages of UP as being for a client?
Having the right talent for the challenge at hand is obviously a huge advantage, especially for clients who've become chagrined with the previous agency model in which talents come and go. In my opinion, an agency is only as good as the team it puts in front of a client.

Size isn't important for UP because the team that works on an account for a client expands and contracts as it's needed. We can also take on as many projects as the largest agency in any given week and deliver by placing work with our pool of members. This ability to grow and shrink impacts back on cost. And UP doesn't have expensive offices in prime locations that need to be paid for no matter what. Our Creative Space concept works far better.

Obviously, we know big companies feel secure dealing with big agencies, but there's a sweet spot with UP that is medium-sized organisations. As the cloud becomes more established, and bigger companies use it more, I'm sure more will come to us.

Project turnaround is also a factor. I handle projects in which UP members in different parts of the world hand elements on to each other around the clock. For instance, a copywriter working in Holland sends brochure copy to a designer in America who produces visuals overnight and passes them back to me to send to the client for checking. Two days' work in 24 hours. Execution times are unbelievable!

UP is also a new agency (and concept) and, as legendary ad man David Ogilvy pointed out, the great thing about a new agency is they're willing to jump through hoops of fire to make their name.

How does being a member of UP benefit individuals?
We know that being online allows us to reinforce and even create our personal brand – look at Facebook. UP members can do this within the community, and they can harness the force of the community to get work for themselves.

I think the secret to a satisfying working life comes down to getting what you're good at, how you make your money and what you want to do in balance. UP allows people to get that balance right. We can stick to the work we like to do – writing, design, whatever – or we can become micro-entrepreneurs winning clients and building our own teams to deliver projects. It's completely up to us.

In the end, it's more about the community offering the opportunity to build teams that are rock solid, backed up with all of the security and online resources to deliver. No one within UP has to be an island. It's pretty much like kids playing League of Legends online!

If the cloud is the future, how do you see that future (pro and con)?
There's no limit to when you can work – which, when it comes to work-life balance is a pro and a con. But it's up to the individual to get that right.

The cloud has the potential to empower the individual who specialises in a particular skill or service. Specialisation is the ultimate driver of quality: it always breeds excellence.

I think it's Thomas Friedman who argues that the individual will become more dominant in the twenty-first century. I'm sure he's right and I'm all for as much individual freedom as possible. But the key thing for me is that the cloud is connecting us in different ways and enabling us to build global communities with shared values and vision.

And we should never forget that we live in a real world of real people in real communities on a real planet that we need to look after. Working in the cloud means not having to commute to offices, being able to get our work-life balance right for the benefit of our families, schools and the communities we're part of, and living where and how we want to. It's long been recognised that mobility is a key generator of wealth.

What has being part of UP and working in the cloud meant for your quality of life?
I've been able to spend a lot more time with my own family, which has made a profound difference. Before becoming part of UP, I was travelling constantly, burning a lot of fossil fuels. And I'm earning more money than ever before!

One unexpected benefit has been the power of the cloud to help me simplify my life. I never have to archive anything on paper and I can find what I want, whenever I want it, wherever I am. All I need is an Internet connection. Nice and tidy.

The one thing is that I never really stop working. But I had the same problem in the old world. It's simply part of the choice I've made.

Really, I'm in a great space.

> *If you build it...*
>
> *Field of Dreams*
> *(Movie), 1989*

Chapter #7
Community

It´s not how big you are...

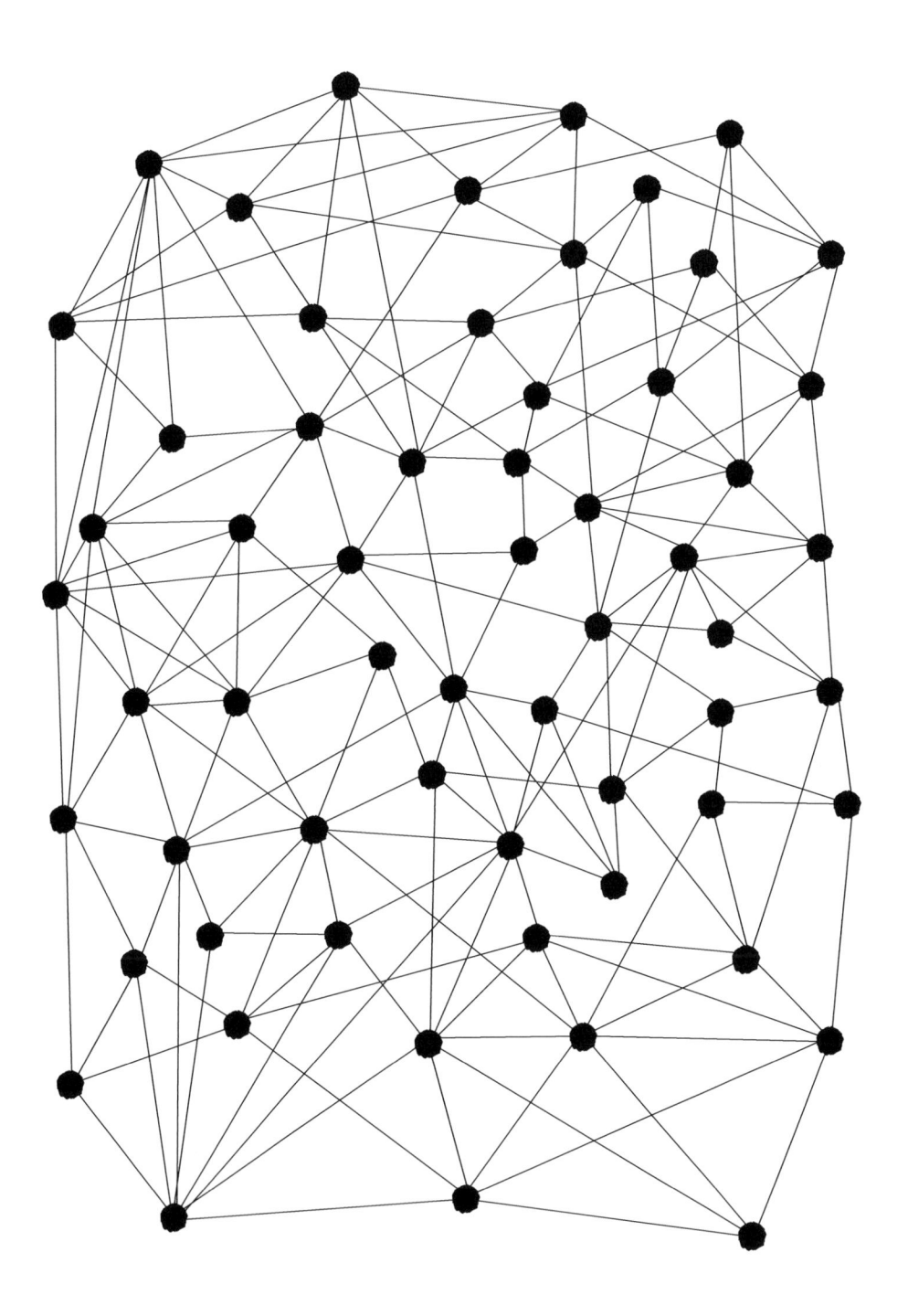

It's how connected you are. It's about community.

"So what exactly are we creating"? Eric asked one day while we were kicking around our new idea on iChat.

We were both excited, because if working in the way we pictured could be great for us, there was no reason why it wouldn't be the same for people we knew in our industry. It had dawned on us that we were building something. But, as you can see from Eric's question, we weren't sure what.

"What do you mean"? I said.

"Is it a network"?

"Can't stand that word. A network is like my LinkedIn list – 1,500 people I don't honestly know that well".

"Is it a virtual…"?

"Can't stand that word either - anything with the word virtual in it is not real enough. And that suggests it's all about the technology, which it isn't. It's about what the technology can do for people."

"Is it a", he paused. "I'm not sure about this, but is it a community"?

I grinned. "Yes" I said. "That's exactly what it is. It's about community".

"Why"? he asked.

"Give me some time to figure it out and I'll tell you why", I said.

I wasn't sure why, but Eric saying the word "community" made me realise what it was that really had been missing in my work life. (18)

***

If we really were building a community, we needed to know what one actually was.
    According to Wikipedia the word "community" comes from the old French "communité", which is itself derived from the Latin "communitas" – cum, which means with or together plus munus, or gift. I take this to mean a group of people coming together because they have something extra to offer each other and the outside world that is more than the sum total of its parts, as they say. This was

our concept in a nutshell.

Our vision of what we wanted to build fit perfectly with the classical definition of a real-world community by German sociologist Ferdinand Tönnies in 1887. According to Tönnies, communities are successful because they combine a "unity of will". This unity could come from being a family or because they share characteristics like religious beliefs.

(Let's not forget that the earliest businesses were built on the strongest possible ties: first of family, then of religion, and often of both. Think of the great businesses like Cadbury, the British chocolate manufacturer started by a Quaker – a religious non-conformist named John Cadbury who opened his first shop in Birmingham, England in 1824. The Protestant faith was very much part of the industrial revolution, which laid the foundations for today's business world. It's called the Protestant Work Ethic for a reason.)

The people who would be part of what we were building would only come together because of this "unity of will". They would understand the benefits of being able to give each other work and form teams to deliver this to clients. These would be people who want to work in teams on client projects and want the chance to work on bigger projects than they could probably tackle on their own.

Communities also stand or fall according to the extent to which people feel a sense of belonging. In their 1986 study of communities, McMillan and Davis define belonging as a "shared emotional connection".

Now emotion might seem a strange thing to bring into play when you're developing a business idea, but I know from my work with brands that it's probably the most powerful force there is. Brands succeed when they make emotional connections that they can back up with services or products that meet real, or created needs.

Corporations also need to create a sense of belonging among employees. Unfortunately, they all too often draw on this emotional bond, but when it comes to the bottom line, a sense of belonging goes out the window. But today's successful businesses – Google and Apple are the first to come to mind – are fantastic at creating a strong and genuine sense of belonging in their employees. (By the way, the other factors McMillan and Davis identified were membership, influence, integration and fulfillment of needs.)

For us to be successful then, we needed to create a sense of belonging among our people. But based on what? The opportunity to work on projects that are interesting, with people who are good at what they do and for clients who are great. But it would have to be more than that. We wondered if there were other people like us who were successful on their own, or even within a conventional organisation, but who wanted to be part of something different, new and better. Together as equals. We were pretty sure there were.

We realised that what we were aiming for was "true community" (19), which is all about developing deep respect and really listening to the needs of the other people in the community.

Once a "true community" is established, strong freedom and security exist – the security to feel free – and people are comfortable enough to get along. This is when a community takes on a life of its own and "social capital" begins to be created. The writer Robert D. Putnam defines social capital as "the inclinations that arise…to do things for each other" (20). Or, in a word, goodwill.

This is what exists in the real world community I'm part of where I live in Sweden. Because we all love where we live and value our community, we have huge amounts of goodwill, manifested in various ways. For instance, my family takes our turn cleaning up the shore of the lake near our house. But in a real world community, you don't get to choose who is a member. You're part of the community whether you like it or not.

About three years ago I went back to see my folks in Cheltenham, the pretty spa town in Gloucestershire, England, where I'm from. I climbed in the back of a cab, gave the driver directions and sat back.

"All right Stubbsy"? the driver said.

I peered at the pair of eyes examining me in the rearview mirror. "Um…It's Keith isn't it? How you doing"?

"Driving a cab now".

"Right, of course".

Keith had been an old school friend that I hadn't seen in 20 years. He had also been the smartest kid in my class.

Keith squinted in the mirror again. With a slightly patronising air he said "Still on the bikes then, Stubbsy"?

Before I'd left Cheltenham I'd been a mad keen motorcyclist. I was confused for a moment and then I realised Keith was talking about my leather jacket which was, incidentally, a Belstaff, which is a rather trendy Italian brand made to make city slickers like me look like real bikers. I didn't say anything.

"Where you living now, Stubbsy"? Keith asked.

"Sweden", I replied, not without a hint of smugness I must admit.

"Ah, Swindon"? he said. "I went there once, didn't like it. The apple doesn't fall far from the tree does it"?

I opened my mouth to correct him and then closed it again without saying anything. Swindon is just 50 miles from Cheltenham.

To the people I grew up with in Cheltenham, I was always going to be part of their community. I was always going to be Stubbsy, who rode around on a motorbike. Which, to be honest, was one of the reasons I felt I had to move on.

But something in me obviously still clearly wanted to belong to something. The difference was, I wanted to create what I was part of. I wanted the choice.

In cyberspace - the fifth dimension we now inhabit - the beauty is that we get to choose who becomes a member of our community. (While this is great, one of the things we discovered early on with UP is that choosing who becomes a member of the community is an art in itself. It's easy to make mistakes. More about the type of people you need to build a great community later.)

Back to social capital. Without social capital communities cannot exist. So we needed to find a way to build social capital into the community we were going to build. We soon realised that to create a sense of belonging and to enable social capital to grow, two things had to happen.

The community had to have a strong leader, able to put his or her ego to one side, to be strategic, to inspire trust, to listen and act decisively. I had the feeling that this was going to be me. Whenever we work together, Eric and I naturally adopt the roles of me as front man – the face, if you like – and him as the guy who really makes things happen, become reality. It was happening again.

I didn't mind leading our community, but what I wanted to happen was to create a community of leaders, with the systems that create a frame that directs how we work (remember Poka Yoke).

Remember, I didn't want to be a boss.

Next, we had to have the systems in place. We needed shared tools for running projects globally, with the ability to store and share files seamlessly wherever we were in the world. We also needed to guarantee a steady flow of communication with members to share our ideas, values and stories, and to enable people to establish their own identities and learn to function within the group. Don't forget, many of the people we were thinking about had been successful freelancers for most of their working lives. We had to make sure the sense of belonging we created and communicated was stronger than their training to be a lone wolf.

In our case, this would mean more than just a Facebook page, it also involved setting up the systems needed to enable members to share projects and to give clients confidence. This was where Eric would come in.

A shared purpose, a real sense of belonging, strong leadership, effective communication and the right tools. If we had these, we could create our community. But why would these win us clients?

Apart from all the benefits of working only in the cloud, Eric and I believed that it was precisely the sense of belonging and the loyalty our community members would inevitably feel for each other that would be our strength.

We would be working for each other as much as we would be servicing a client. Now that was really powerful.

Oh, and we needed a name.

We'd been kicking around the name the Fourth Cloud for a while and rather liked it. We'd even dummied up a logotype and business card. We were just about to apply for a trademark registration when I found a similar company with the same name in Canada. I knew that as we would become increasingly global it would eventually become a problem. I was in Stockholm that night, staying at the small overnight apartment we owned. My wife and I went to a local restaurant and I was feeling rather concerned over the name issue. I have the habit of scribbling to think. I scribbled the now defunct name The Fourth Cloud on the paper tablecloth. Underneath this I wrote the tagline I'd been playing around with. UP THERE, EVERYWHERE.

My wife leaned over and said, "Actually I think the tagline is the best bit". I scratched out the original name and looked at UP THERE, EVERYWHERE.

"You're right", I said, "It is". She does this to me on a regular basis. Just when I think I've been brilliant, I realise it's actually her that is brilliant.

From that moment we became UP THERE, EVERYWHERE – the global cloud-based agency.

Community

e-ployment

Interview with Simon Cohen
by David Holzer, UP member

Simon Cohen describes himself as:
An optimistic young man, a person on a spiritual journey, a silly dancer, a writer and thinker, someone who tries to communicate with conscience, which is a daily journey, a slightly moaning vegetarian (I miss meat but couldn't possibly think of eating it) all round nice chap, founder of global tolerance, daddy to be, broadcaster, public speaker, moral and social commentator.

As usual, he's being rather modest. See what I mean at mrsimoncohen.com. I talked to Simon specifically because one of the things we at UP all share is a desire to make a difference by working differently. Simon's perspective on our responsibilities in the "real world" is one I personally share.

We started off by talking about how Simon works and his view of working in an office or, as he puts out, out of the office.

* * *

Do you work in an office or from home?
Life has changed quite a bit for me recently. I put my ethical communications company, global tolerance, on a year's sabbatical, after nine years, and right now I'm working at home two days a week. In the cloud.

Do you have a preference?
There are different constituent parts of both experiences to consider. The journey to the office can be positive or negative, depending on the interactions along the way, how long it takes and the opportunity cost of the journey.

And there's the type of office. Office can be quite a broad concept. global tolerance was based on a World War I era ship on London's River Thames, so we worked to the sound of waves lapping against the ship and looked out the portholes at the light shining on the water. It was a positive, empowering, soothing environment.

I also have a very soothing, lovely environment at my home in Brighton, on the southern coast of the UK. I get to look out the window at the sea and occasionally at my computer.

I'd say that when I factor in things like being present for my wife and baby I prefer home. But for a creative dynamic and communicating with bodies and not just hands and eyes, I prefer being out of home.

What do you think of when you hear the words "online community"?
My instant response is "offline community", because an online community is only as strong as its ability to complement and benefit offline relationships in the real world, or it's just ego massaging. Equally, an offline community has to benefit from the richness of online experiences and relationships. It's about symbiosis, which both communities need to develop a real sense of community. An online community that stands for the exclusion of the offline world is obviously oxymoronic.

What do you think makes a strong online community?
I think that first and foremost communities are built through an understanding of the deep needs of those invited to be part of them. Some are just set up with a lick of a finger in the air and guesswork as to the needs of the people asked to join.

Here's an example of an online community that I think really works. I'm going to be a dad. So I sent out a tweet to mums.net asking them if they can give me any advice in 140 characters or less. In the past hour I've received 30 replies.

mums.net is successful because it has a deep understanding of its community, taps into a need and, by its very nature, provides mutual aid between an online and offline community. The people who set it up have gone through what members are experiencing so there's already an empathic and compassionate connection between community builders and the member base. For instance, the builders know that among the concerns of new parents are being cut off socially from friends and family, having less time and less sleep. It really comes down to answering the question, "How do I feel connected as a human being"?

mums.net meets a deep spiritual need and, because of this, it has a disproportionate chance of succeeding. That need is not going to go away any time soon.

What do you think online communities have the potential to do?

Build or break the universe as we know it. Look at what Facebook and Twitter did as part of the Arab Spring, helping to take down a 30-year dictatorship in a matter of weeks.

Or, look at the financial markets, which are based on confidence more than anything else. Confidence stems from information and a viewpoint flowing from people we trust. Online communities are absolutely central to building or breaking the confidence and financial flow.

On a micro level, online communities have the potential to help us be all we can be, to refine and reframe our thoughts with friends and fellow travellers online and bring them to life in the real world. And when thoughts, words and deeds are aligned, this is what many call enlightenment or success. It's my personal goal. So online communities are a fantastic tool that simply were not around 20 or so years ago.

What do you think is the immediate future for employment for skilled professionals?

As a man in his early 30s who has hired and let go a number of people over the past nine years, my experience is that professionals tend to fit into two categories.

One is a type of personality that loves structure, processes and a framework in which to work. These are the people who will leave university and lap up graduate placement schemes that have them photocopying for weeks on end. They're happy knowing what they're doing, receiving a salary and having a pension scheme. When those things are taken away it's panic stations.

The other category is, broadly, a bit more entrepreneurial and rejects traditional ideas of security. The people in this category are proactive and responsive and see lack of processes, structures and systems as an opportunity to leave an indelible mark on life. Working differently, they begin to pioneer.

In my opinion, the traditional definitions of security and success are obsolete. Of course, some people will always need to go to a big shiny office because it's a symbol of security. Working for a company with a well-known brand is also a symbol of status, success and position.

But, increasingly, because there's a shifting tide in consciousness towards nurturing the whole human being through employment and not just factoring them into an equation, there is an increasing number of people who are beginning to question the traditional metrics for success. These people actually see themselves as more successful if they only have to commute for five minutes, if they commute at all, and can spend lunch on the beach with good people.

So, demand by these people for a new way of working means supply will need to shift. But it's a question of swimming against the tide of commerce at the moment, because a private legal entity distributing profit among shareholders has to put that before philosophy.

I consider myself one of the most successful business people around, but if someone were to look at what I took home last year they'd probably laugh their socks off.

And it comes down to trust. You're only empowered to be innovative when you've got a basis of trust. What the debate triggered by Marissa Mayer, CEO of Yahoo!, when she forced employees to come back to the office, demonstrated to me was that Yahoo! didn't trust the people who worked for the company.

When trust and relationships aren't there, that's when we have insecurity. We're nervous and unsure of the people we have on board and believe we need to be physically together to talk it through. For me, if you feel you can only stay connected if you're all in the office together than you're in more trouble than you thought.

What do you think of the concept of an online community business like UP?
Time will tell whether this is just a great business idea or a good idea for the world. Clearly, in unpredictable economic times it makes eminent sense to reduce overheads: no centralized office, no payroll, just a committed group of professionals. These are all ingredients for traditional business success. The challenge as I see it, and this is a challenge I share with global tolerance as well, is to be really ruthlessly honest about the motivations for our actions.

There's something called a lifestyle business. Is this a model that supports and embraces its community members' lifestyles and enables them to have a quality of life that they're attracted to. I don't think there's any question that this is the case for UP, but is it more than that?

In order for UP to be a good idea for the world, the values, vision and motivations of the business for the world need to shine through, and the greatest opportunity for these to shine through lies in the community itself. Will the conversation about the big questions happen within the community and does success look beyond the bottom line alone?

I hope so.

> *I don't see $4.00 in Starbucks as an expensive coffee. I see it as a cheap office*
>
> Eric Dowell,
> Co-Founder UP

Chapter #8

The time bandit

24/7

/365

It's 9 o' clock somewhere — someone's always UP

Although Eric and I were united in imagining a different take on a conventional start-up, we still faced the usual challenges: find people, put systems in place, create a great name for the organisation and, above all, win clients. You haven't heard from him yet, so I'll let Eric tell the next part of the story.

This section I've called the time bandit because that's Eric's nick name. He's simply the most productive creative person I've ever met in my life – and I've met a few. He's a machine. He adds an extra dimension when it comes to time. He's also brilliant when it comes to designing systems to make our time more productive. Time that can hopefully lead to a better work, life balance.

Anyway, over to Eric.

***

Julian and I felt like kids again, driving each other on to build our vision of what our business could be. We knew it was a great idea, with so much potential and a very dynamic way of working, but there was a lot we had to do to get the thing off the ground.

Because we were imagining something that hadn't been done before, we were in uncharted territory, which added an exciting dimension but also made us a little nervous.

At this early stage, we were pretty sure we knew the advantages the technology could deliver. We were going to be global and send projects back and forth across time zones, working around the clock between us to deliver projects in at least half the time it would take a conventional agency.

We also understood that because we didn't need offices we could obviously dramatically reduce overhead costs; tools like iChat and Skype, our main method of communication, were relatively cheap. So we could be ultra-competitive.

The real challenge we faced in the early days was finding the people with all the different skill sets we needed, and the faith in what we were proposing, to come together.

Both Julian and I believed that, although our industry had splintered into various different disciplines, the value we offered was our ability to determine which of these was right for what our clients wanted to achieve.

First of all, we had to decide what we were actually offering the people that we wanted to join our new community. It boiled down to the opportunity for them to keep their independence while being able to call on the skills of specialists and the resources of a large organisation backed by a solid brand. People would make a contribution to the cost of building the organisation in the form of working for the community to help it, and them, grow.

In our experience, "freelancers" (detest that word) tended to charge whatever they could get away with because they knew the agency they were working for would mark their costs up substantially.

If we all kept our costs competitive and realistic, we could help each other do well and, just as importantly, build bonds of trust.

We decided very early on that we were building an organisation of members, people who subscribed to the same ideas. I absolutely agreed with Julian that "no offices, no employees, just people" was our mantra.

Once we knew what we were offering, we started by approaching the people we knew who were experts in disciplines that were a necessary part of what we wanted to offer clients: digital media, social media and PR, for instance. You'll hear from some of these people later on.

Apart from how good they were at what they did, these were all people who had never let us down. In our industry, once you accept a job, you've just got to do it. But when you take away a rigid, hierarchical management structure, which was what we were proposing, what was going to be the driver for the people we recruited?

It turned out to be character. Character is something that really resonates in the cloud.

Right from the start, it was clear that the people who took wings right away were those who didn't need to be told what to do and who delivered on time, in whatever way it took. To be honest, that was kind of what we expected. The people who agreed to join us had all been freelance for a number of years and were used to working that way. The most important word in their, and our, vocabulary was self-responsibility.

Like us, part of what appealed to these people was the opportunity to belong to something without being chained to it. They knew they could do big things as an individual, but far bigger things as a group. A group wins out over an individual every time.

They were also people who were determined to get their work-life balance right but who also knew that the days of working nine-to-five were long gone. Although they had been freelance for a number of years, which meant they were pretty much in a certain age bracket, let's just say, the people who signed up understood that they would have to re-educate themselves constantly to keep up with what the technology enables. They were people who were flexible and adaptable enough to be comfortable in the cloud. They could think for themselves.

(They were also people like me who'd long ago abandoned the idea of working in an office. I've been using coffee shops as temporary offices for a while now and, for me, it's great. When people complain about the cost of a cup of coffee at Starbucks, my answer is that it's a cheap price to pay to be catered to and connected. As UP evolves, we're incorporating real-world Creative Spaces and meeting places into our vision, but by no stretch of the imagination are these offices. We're redefining the work space in the same way as we're redefining our business.)

But what was more surprising was the way in which some people immediately understood that this was their chance to unleash their own entrepreneurial spirit. They realised that they could join us and have the opportunity to share a piece of a business, and offer other members with specialist skills the chance to be involved. Overnight they could be off and running, without losing any of their independence.

Now we had the people, we were collaborating and scratching each other's backs and we grew pretty rapidly. By the end of the first year UP totaled 40 people, in ten locations. But it turned out that the technological side of things was a little more of a challenge than we'd initially thought.

We began to see some pitfalls in our model.

* * *

As we began to grow, which happened very fast, I started to see that our potential Achilles heel was going to be the amount of paperwork that would be generated because of the way we worked with people. There were lots of issues at the back end involving the sheer volume of invoices being shuffled. Someone's got to ask the questions: is this the right amount, did this invoice go out, did these people get paid?

If we'd been building a traditional business, we'd simply have offered someone a job, signed a contract with them, and they would have been paid monthly or whatever. It's straightforward. Our members would remain self-employed, handling their own tax obligations in their own countries so we wouldn't have to worry about that side of things. But we still had to make sure all the invoices we received were in the correct amount, with the necessary information and assigned to the right project. One person could easily do 30 to 40 jobs a year for us, which meant a lot of invoices to be managed.

By default, it's safe to say that I became the systems guy. (Maybe it's worth mentioning here that my dad was an engineer with NASA, and I must have inherited some of his genes.) One of my jobs was to make sure the systems we had in place were both robust enough and that we adhered to them. We also had to make sure the data we collected was always available in the cloud, where anyone who had to access it could do so. After a lot of research, I finally realised that we had to have a data management system custom-designed to our business model.

We needed to make sure all the data was collected automatically in the cloud where anyone could see it; people like the account manager.

I like these kinds of challenges so I found it exciting. Especially when it occurred to us that by building this system and overcoming these challenges we were essentially creating a great product that we could then sell to other businesses that wanted to operate in the cloud. Or we could offer it to organisations we simply wanted to help. Doing good and making a difference was an important part of our vision from the start. But, before we move on, a slight digression into the subject of the cloud and security.

* * *

In an interview with Stanley Bing in this book, he questions, in his usual entertainingly provocative way, how secure the cloud is.

Now, I've done a lot of research on the cloud, and all of the evidence suggests that we are a lot safer putting our data up there than storing it on our own computers. We may lose our individual hard drives but we can always access data in the cloud.

And, one of the things about the age we're living in now is that access to content and data is in hyperdrive. Everything is copied and copied, so it's always backed up and available somewhere.

As for servers that are located in Silicon Valley, near the San Andreas fault, or are vulnerable to natural catastrophes like Hurricane Sandy, my impression of the guys in Silicon Valley is that those companies really live it. They cover any angle. So they don't just have one server. Data is scattered about. Those companies have made sure that if they're attacked it won't make any difference. To me, the Internet world is highly stable. As for the question of the security of data based in the cloud we test it repeatedly to ensure all our data is secure and backed-up. With the large graphic and film files we store we even have the ability to back-track (go back in time) and retrieve historical data from the previous day, or week etc. Fantastic!

There's no question that the cloud is here to stay and will continue to grow. Competition as to who provides the cloud will certainly increase as international providers take their share of the cloud pie, perhaps capitalising on fears that the NSA is looking at data. I can imagine closed national clouds coming into being for security reasons. In fact, I'm sure the cloud security industry will expand exponentially, which will benefit all of us.

The only risk I can see is governments enacting laws to restrict the international use of the cloud in the same way some have tried to restrict access to content on the web. I hope that won't happen. Slowing down the process of people around the globe working together is to the detriment of a better planet.

* * *

So, back to the building of our own system. We found our development partner in Dropbox, Inc., which offers cloud storage, file synchronisation and client software and sign-up for their its cloud-based server. We'd been one of the earliest users of Dropbox and when we really looked into it, we saw that the concept was solid and we believed the company was going to lead the way.

Working with Dropbox, we've tried to anticipate as many problems as we can. For instance, we soon understood that one of the things that's essential for us is keeping track of files and sharing them as needed. If people weren't around anymore, we needed to know everything they had worked on.

With Dropbox, any file that has been put up in the cloud is always accessible. We can turn the clock back on any individual job and recover the related files that were created.

Phew.

* * *

Today, looking back on the first couple of years of UP, it's fantastic to see that the joint vision Julian and I had, shared by the people who've joined UP, is really working. We're running rings around other traditional agencies because of the advantages of working in the cloud, combined with the quality of the people who are part of UP. I would say it's because all of us are loyal to each other and we see the benefits - financial and otherwise - of being part of a group or community of people we know and trust. We quickly became far more than just a bunch of freelancers working together; we are a community. We're also hungry. We want to succeed, but we also want to prove that our idea really works. We're champions of a new concept, if you like. It was seeing this hunger and sense of community that made me realise that something special was going on.

We employ nobody and yet we win business. I'm really intrigued about how that's going to influence the future of employment. That's a great joy for me and there's a real thrill in that. It's interesting and exciting and I'd say other people are catching on too slowly. It amazes me that they're still working in the old-world ways while we're running UP with a totally new model.

We're also part of a movement to change the way work works. Because the world is getting smaller, borders between countries and states are no longer as important. This is an opportunity for pay levels to equalise across the globe, for great people to prosper wherever they are in the world, and for them to remain a vital part of their real-world communities.

I've been responsible for the development of our biggest investment to date – the SUPER System. SUPER is our own, custom-designed administrative and finance system. It cost a cool quarter of a million dollars and will be worth wevery cent. It's a fully automated cloud-based accounting system that will allow us to grow much more rapidly in the next five years. SUPER is the missing piece and a really exciting step. And, we're inventing it, which is really cool.

For me, there's no limit to how large the movement can grow. The dynamic of this is that profound. We're part of the move to do something great by envisioning an opportunity around the way the world is getting very small.

The time bandit

Interview with a corporate home worker, who wished to remain anonymous. So let's just call him Brian
by David Holzer, UP member

The realities of life for a corporate home worker.
Brian works 100% from home for a global organisation in the IT industry as a contractual home worker. I talked to him about what it's really like to work in this way.

How did you become a home worker?
I chose to do it. I absolutely didn't want to work in an office again. Before becoming a home worker I worked in local government in the UK for over 15 years. An office is great for young people, but I really didn't like it – the way you had to put on a social face, always make allowances for relationships and not just do your work. I was sick and tired of the physical act of going into the office, so I was really happy when I no longer had to go into one.

What was it like when you started home working?
There was the culture shock of starting to work from home. For the first few weeks it was weird. I wondered what I'd done.

There was an assumption at the beginning from my family that I could do all the household chores, go grocery shopping and so on. They also didn't realise that even though I was at home I was fully at work, so they made all the noise they normally would.

And now?
After six years I'm used to it. I wouldn't say it's really flexible for me, but it's a price worth paying not to have to be in the office. And my family understands the way it works now.
It hasn't really improved my work-life balance but that doesn't really have to do with home working, it's more to do with working for a large corporation. I work a ten-hour day on average. It's the nature of the job and of working for a global corporation. But I still would rather be at home than in an office.

For a corporation, what do you think are the advantages of having home workers?

Corporations know that it's all about managing people on output – I supervise a team and I know that. Clearly, the majority of people are conscientious and will do what's expected and more. They're also worried people will think they're not pulling their weight. They know people are waiting for them to deliver and conscious when they don't.

So it's not actually about cost. For my employers, the financial model of home working doesn't actually work, as they've discovered. There's no linear relationship between people working from home and reducing costs. A building has still got to be paid for, whether there are one or 100 people in it.

Home working also doesn't reduce the need for travel for me. If I have to meet someone face to face, I have to. It's as simple as that.

That's why it's really about productivity. Here's another example. I've been home working for six years now. In that time I would have probably had 50 or so sick days. Instead I've had about five since I started home working.

And the future?
I'm a home worker until I retire.

> *Some people believe football is a matter of life and death, I am very disappointed with that attitude. I can assure you it is much, much more important than that*
>
> Bill Shankly,
> *manager of Liverpool Football Club 1959 - 1974*

Chapter #9

Work, life and balance

work
life

balance

I think all of us who are looking for new ways to work and live come to the inescapable conclusion that we need to re-balance our entire lives in some way. This section touches on this topic. In truth it deserves a whole book in itself. Finding a new way to work and live however, is the most important step you'll ever take.

Four years ago I decided to step out of "normal employment" from a very well paid job to take control of my own life again. Like anything worth doing it evoked a mix of feelings. Excitement, challenge and fear in equal parts probably, but, I guess to feel alive there has to be some element of risk involved. Part of the motivation was to re-balance my life and live the way I really wanted to live. Money is an important consideration in all this obviously, but that's where the re-balancing comes in. How much do you really need and is just earning money alone the most important thing in your life? I have friends in the US who often ask why I haven't moved there, after all, salaries in my profession are much higher and tax is certainly a lot lower than in Sweden. Well, I'm not ruling it out in the future, as I'd rather like the experience, but for me at the moment it's a matter of quality of life. Sweden offers me, and most importantly my family, a great quality of life. Don't get me wrong – I like money as much as anyone and I'm a proponent of Groucho Marx's view:

> *While money can't buy happiness, it certainly lets you choose your own form of misery*
>
> *Groucho Marx*

So what is balance about? Maybe it's about the balance between work and life? Well, even that is a complex issue.

I started this section with a quote from one of my personal heroes, Bill Shankly, for two simple reasons. Firstly, it's my book. Secondly, that quote really exemplifies the most important ingredient in work and life. Passion. If you have passion for what you do it's no longer work. Without passion everything is just a slog. A daily grind. People who go to work for eight hours a day and hate it, are worse off in my opinion than someone who works 10, 12 or even 16 hours a day and loves what they do.

I struggle to separate work and life and I've come to the conclusion it's just not my view of the world. I really love what I'm lucky enough to work with, so it's no longer work, but is an important element of my total life. The two go hand in hand.

So what is balance all about for me? It's about getting a balance in the time I spend in my professional life and the time I have with my family and friends. E-Ployment allows me the freedom to maximise and balance these.

For around ten years I used to sit in a car for up to three hours a day on my daily commute to reach an office where I would sit for eight to 10 hours a day with a group of other people who were all making similar treks. I figured out that the three hour commute was an almost total loss in terms of productivity. The fuel used by my car was a waste and the pollution it pumped out was harming the environment. The three hour commute time was also time sacrificed with my family. That's 15 hours a week which equates to a whopping 30 days a year for me. Even if you gain only half that time in a year, that's like having an extra two weeks a year for vacation with your family. Do the arithmetic on your own commuting time and ask yourself what it costs you every year.

The sheer waste of my old commute now seems like total madness. Imagine if more people were able to embrace E-Ployment and be even more productive and get more time with their family. Doesn't seem like a bad idea to me.

E-Ployment allows me to get more out of everyday and work as hard as I like, as well as spend maximum time with my family. If I want to play football with my son at 3pm in the afternoon, I'll do it. If I have to work from 8pm to midnight to buy that time I'll do that as well. It's my decision and I take self-responsibility for that (more on that later).

Taking charge
The other really important thing I do with my time is to focus on me. Now this seems a bit selfish, but it's in fact really important. It's something we all need to do – spend some time with ourselves. As I've said earlier in this book being self-employed is a bit like being a mini managing director. A managing director in charge of yourself. It's the most important job you'll ever get. Treat yourself as

a small corporation and think about all the important departments you have to run and organise. Obviously sales and administration is key. Training and HR are really important as well. But right at the top of the list is employee health. The need to keep yourself healthy and fit both physically and mentally.

In the past I've struggled to manage this aspect well. Like many people, it always seems the easiest thing to sacrifice when time is tight, just skip taking some physical exercise. Well this, along with some mental exercise time, is really the most valuable time of each day.

As managing director in charge of yourself take the decision to set time aside everyday from here on in for yourself. Amazingly, you don't even lose any time as I can guarantee it will make you more productive and keep you in the best condition. As a mini managing director it's the best investment you'll ever make in your corporation. Find the right time that works best for you everyday. This will obviously be different for different people. I'm an early bird and normally wake around 5:30am. For me that's the best time of the day to get some exercise. So I try to make the early morning my time and I always feel like I get a head start on the day. But we're all different so find the time that suits you best, and make it your own.

So how much time does it take to keep yourself mentally and physically fit?

In my case I have been following the advice of my close friend and personal trainer Niki Tramentana. He's taken a complete view of my life and profession and come up with a personalised programme that suits me. It's based on good nutrition, getting plenty of rest, as well as exercise. That last one is based on what's called Tabata training. Short, intense, exercises that are really effective. Totally time? 15 minutes a day. I also practise something they call "vita månader" in Swedish. But I'll let Niki talk about that and how to take charge of health.

Work, life and balance

Interview

Interview with Nikola Tramontana. Niki runs FORM, Training and Fitness Centre, in the town of Knivsta, just outside of Uppsala, Sweden. He's a personal trainer, practises naprapathy and is simply a genius when it comes to the body and health.

Niki – what is your typical client like?
Well I guess all sorts of people, but nowadays many are people with hectic business and personal lives who are looking to turn the clock back 10 or 20 years and get themselves back into good shape again. They still have to manage their work lives of course, so I like to talk to my clients about becoming fit for business. Become a business athlete by managing their energy.

So where should we start in getting ourselves fit again?
We don't get the free time to do the things we love and when we do find some space we have no energy left to fully enjoy the moment. It's a vicious cycle that's easy to get trapped within.

Too many people tend to spend their time recovering from life instead of living it. This is caused by a mix of stress combined with deadlines and informational overload all of which drains our system of energy. We become tired on a "cellular" level. So we have to start on a cellular level when we want to find the right solution for gaining more energy.

What are the steps?
There are some really simple steps, but it all starts with creating a good physiological environment and then the rest will follow.

You have to focus on where energy is created in our bodies. It's in the cell. Give the cell the best environment through good nutrition, good sleep and allowing sufficient recovery time.
Think of it this way. When you eat the wrong things or go to bed too late you're putting bad energy into your body. Bad energy 'in' almost certainly means you will get bad energy 'out'! You probably won't feel great.

So start to really think about what you are eating. Good food practise is extremely important and actually pretty simple. Start with eating real, wholesome, food. Aim to cut out all processed foods – or food that has been manufactured in some way. Studies show that four of the top ten chronic diseases, such as heart disease, diabetes, strokes and cancer, can be traced directly to the industrialisation of our food. Cut all refined sugars and starches. Finally don't use any artificial preservatives or sweeteners. Just focus on proper food as it should be.

Next give your body a break from alcohol. Again it has been linked to major chronic diseases and can have an immediate and negative impact on the body. If you want to enjoy an occasional drink do so, but keep it in moderation. In Sweden we have something we call "vita månader" or "white months". These are complete months without alcohol. It allows your body to recover and gives your system a break, which is a really smart idea.

Finally, think about taking regular exercise. The benefits can be seen really quickly and can have a dramatic impact on your metabolism. Taking exercise helps lower your stress hormones, improves problem solving abilities and memory, as well as helps keep blood sugar levels in far better balance.
Added to this it will give you increased energy as well as help improve the quality of your sleep.

But how long should we spend exercising?
That's the really great thing. Modern research has shown we can achieve huge health benefits in a fairly short amount of time. For people who lead really busy lives I'd recommend they look at the Tabata training method. This focuses on high intensity interval training, where in just a short

space of time, say just ten minutes a day, people can achieve the same impact as a forty minute session in the gym. Look it up online.

Training is not about how many hours you spend in the gym anymore. It's about what you do in the time that you are there. Being fast, simple and effective is the key!

Finally what do you think about E-Ployment?
I think society needs to find new ways to help people balance their work and personal lives and people certainly need to maintain a healthy lifestyle. A lot of my clients come to me because they lead stressful, busy, lives and as a result their health suffers. E-Ployment seems to be an alternative way to work and live life and that's something more and more people are looking for nowadays. It has to be a good thing, but it demands self-responsibility.

Thanks Niki. A perfect place to end. Or maybe begin?

> *If you plan on being anything less than you are capable of being, you will probably be unhappy all the days of your life*
>
> Abraham Maslow

Chapter #10

ME ME ME and self-responsibility

It's all about me me me me me me me me me me me me me me me

The key is Self-responsibility

Eric's observation in chapter eight that it's character that makes for an ideal member of UP and, by extension, any similar community-type business or organisation, made me think harder about why we're coming together in the way we are right now.

Apart from all the things I have already described, the fall-out from the global economic crisis, the reaction of corporations and government forcing a growth in self-employment, the power of the cloud – it seems to me that everyone within UP, and our clients, has a certain need that we can help meet.

I'm not talking about the need for economic stability, a better work-life balance and so on. Here it's about something deeper than that.

I'm not a great reader of self-help books and I'm certainly not at all into the New Age movement or whatever it's called today. But when I was introduced to the work of Richard Barrett, and specifically his book The New Leadership Paradigm and website newleadershipparadigm.com, which dares to introduce the concept of the "soul" into the discussion around where business needs to go in the 21st century, it made a lot of sense. (21)

**

I think it's fair to say that Richard's work builds on the pioneering work of the American psychologist Abraham Maslow. Those of us with a background in marketing are bound to be familiar with Maslow's *Hierarchy of Needs.*

Maslow identified five needs that are usually shown in a pyramid.

In ascending order they are:

Physiological needs – food, water, sleep, sex

Safety needs – personal and financial security, health and well-being and protection against accidents or illness and their impact

Love and belonging – friendship, intimacy, family

Esteem – the need to be accepted, valued and respected and to have self-esteem and self-respect

Self-actualisation – realising our full potential, becoming everything we can possibly be

Maslow argues that the first three layers of the pyramid are what he calls "deficiency needs". If these aren't met, we tend to feel anxious. Once they are met, we look towards the top two needs of esteem and self-actualisation.

In my own case, I'd say that, although I've got a long way to go, my work on getting my work-life balance in better shape is a good example of meeting the first of Maslow's needs because I'm healthier. Now that I feel like I'm meeting them, I'm focusing on those higher up the pyramid.

For us marketers, Maslow's Hierarchy of Needs is a great way of identifying needs that the products and services we're tasked with marketing can meet. Of course, we're also in the business of creating need wherever we can, but what we create is still pegged to basic human psychology.

Richard starts with Maslow and goes into fascinating territory that is absolutely relevant for myself, my fellow UP members and, given that you're reading this book, you. It has to be said that I've simplified Richard's arguments and cherry-picked the parts that best fit my argument.

***

Richard suggests that we all possess seven levels of consciousness and presents them in order from higher to lower, as it were. The top four are most relevant for us:

7. Service – you see yourself as a member of the human race and want to achieve a sense of joy in your life by fulfilling your purpose

6. Making a difference – you see yourself as a member of a community and/or affiliated with groups that have shared values, aligned missions and a common vision

5. Internal cohesion – you're a member of group with shared values and a mission aligned with your own sense of purpose and direction

4. Transformation – the group you're a member of, which shares your values and goals, celebrates and encourages your unique abilities and talents. Membership in UP encourages all of these things

***

Richard begins by arguing that the original definition of psychology was not the study of the mind but the study of the soul. Now you may not believe in the concept of a soul, but it's well worth bearing with him.

He starts by making a distinction between the ego and the soul. For Richard, the ego is the part of our personality associated with our body and its day to day needs – Maslow's physiology, security, belonging and self-esteem categories.

Most of us are, for a large part of the time, operate at the ego level of existence. In today's economic climate, and in a world of increasingly rapid change and growing complexity, I would say that's fair enough. But what about the soul?

According to Richard, the soul is the part of our personality associated with what he calls the "energetic human body". That is, everything that isn't our physical body. The soul is searching for meaning and wants to make a difference in the world. Of course, I'm well aware that we can only do this when our basic needs are met.

Whether you choose to call it the soul or not, there's no question that some of us need to make a difference in the world and that's a key aspect of UP. It's one of the things that sets us apart from "talent exchanges", "e-lance" and creative crowdsourcing sites. You already know my opinion on creative crowdsourcing, but it's worth repeating. As far as I can see, it's all about securing the best possible cost no matter what and, in some instances, devaluing what highly skilled writers and designers, in particular, can offer by forcing them to compete against people who live in economies associated with a far lower cost of living. UP gives our clients a great deal, but we also respect the skills of our members and always try and secure a fair rate for their work.

Richard explores some other areas that also have relevance to the UP story. For example, the place of business in the world and the qualities needed to thrive in the new world of work.

* * *

Richards's book is, as the title suggests, all about leadership of self and others. But what he says about the place of business in today's world is, to my mind, absolutely right.

According to Richard, too many of the leaders of our global financial systems and business organisations see themselves as separate from society and community. He gives a specific example: in their personal lives, business people are concerned about the environment, locally and globally, because it impacts back on their children's futures. But when they're in what they view as their business life, the same people put profit first.

They regard business, and themselves as business people, as separate from society. For me, this is not true. As UP evolves, we're realising more and more that another one of our differences is that we see business as, quite simply, people relating to other people.

And one of the interesting things about working online is that the Internet - especially the cloud, because it enables transparency (if people choose to embrace this) - makes it far easier for people within organisations to enter into dialogue with each other directly.

So we value people – our members and our clients - equally, and this is one of the things that is giving us a competitive advantage, especially in a world that appears incredibly turbulent, constantly changing and complex.

To paraphrase something Richard says, "UP is no longer operating in a world of us and them. There's only us".

* * *

I won't go into too much detail, but Richard's observations regarding the power of adaptability are highly relevant for UP and any other organisation considering operating in a similar way.

Richard identifies five characteristics that are essential for evolution.

They are:

Adaptability – the ability of an entity to maintain internal stability and external equilibrium when changes occur in its natural environment

Continuous learning – the power to store what you have learned about how to adapt in your memory and the ability to use what you have learned in the past as a platform for future learning

Ability to bond – for the purpose of mutual survival; this builds resilience, but strong bonds require a high degree of trust

Cooperation – successful cooperation for the purpose of mutual survival, requires alignment of purpose and a high degree of empathy

Ability to handle complexity – how to survive and thrive in increasingly complex framework conditions is at the core of evolution: our ability to handle complexity develops gradually and naturally as we grow older through experience

In Richard's view, evolution proves that adaptability is a more powerful force for change than imposing change (think of water taking the path of least resistance, think of "Poka Yoke") and that bonding and cooperation are at the heart of adaptation.

It goes without saying that bonding and cooperation in the service of the common good, and our clients, are at the heart of UP. We're back to Adam Smith here, with his concept of the "invisible hand" or self-interest. UP is a perfect example of this concept in action.

Let's go back to when Eric and I created UP. We were acting in our own self-interest, and ours was a survival strategy. The way we were working threatened our physical health because our work-life balance was out of whack and we were neither fulfilled nor enjoying ourselves, so we embraced (maybe invented) a way of working that in theory enabled us to improve that balance. And we adapted to it, as did the people who became and are becoming members of UP.

The ability to handle change and complexity is also worthy of comment. At the moment, UP members tend to be more mature (referring to chronological age here). This is because Eric and I are also more mature, and so are the majority of people in our professional networks, the people we initially invited to join UP (I hasten to add that as new members join the age range is falling.)

The fact that UP members are of a certain age, predominantly 35 and upwards is hugely advantageous not just to us but to our clients. We are all people who have had to be able to adapt and handle change and complexity to survive as freelances in our industry for as long as we have. It's second nature for us to think for ourselves, because we've always had to.

We're the people that other people want to work with because they know they can trust us. They know we will take self-responsibility.

And self-responsibility is an important idea to us. At UP we have established a number of values we think are important to the people within the organisation and to our clients in choosing to work with us. We are Collaborative. We work closely with each other and our clients. We involve the client throughout the creative process, and we are never precious about our own ideas being best. We show Respect. Even when we disagree, we always share respect for each other's opinions, and for our clients' professional opinions. We all value Freedom. The freedom to work the way we do, and live the way we want. Positive Passion. UP is a positive word. Anything is possible. UP also has passion. We're in this business because we have a passion for it. Positive Passion drives everything we do. Maintaining Balance. Balance in our own lives as well as in the environment is critical. Balance in our professional view and the client's professional view. Attention to Detail. Ours is a business of big ideas, but as importantly attention to small details. Our clients will always come back to us based on this and the quality of what we deliver. Then we have one driving principle and value that sits above all of this and we think is the most important focus of all. Self-responsibility. This is the most important value we have. At UP THERE, EVERYWHERE we take responsibility for our clients, our colleagues, our business, ourselves, our families, and importantly our planet and its environment. I've always said that the UP model is probably not for everyone or even for all clients. Some people probably need a boss and an office to go to everyday. But I'm not one of them and most of the people like me tend to exhibit a high degree of self-responsibility. The willingness to look after their own lives and the world around them. Really it all comes down to it all being about ME ME ME - not in the selfish sense, but in taking self-responsibility.

But for UP and any organisation like us to make a real lasting difference, we need to attract new blood, the young people who, as Michael Jackson so poetically put it, are "our future". We're in a great position to offer a brighter future to creative, dynamic, driven young people who want to get into our industry globally, something which, at the moment, is extremely hard to do.

So, the next chapter is all about what comes next.

e-ployment

Interview with Stanley Bing
by David Holzer, UP member

I picked up my first copy of the American magazine Esquire in the early 1980s and was hooked right away. I learned how to tie a four-in-hand knot in my yellow polka-dot tie. I found out where Prince of Wales Check came from. I knew where to go for the best martini if I was ever in Memphis. I read great sports writing and excellent short fiction. Best of all, I discovered Stanley Bing.

Before reading Stanley, I'd never thought that the business world and corporate life were worth writing or reading about. Stanley changed all that for me.

Since Esquire, Stanley has written a series of best-selling books including What Would Machiavelli Do?, 100 Bullshit Jobs and How to Get Them and Executricks: How to Retire While You're Still Working.

In 2007, Stanley began a daily blog, www.stanleybing.com, which appears on Fortune's website as well as that of its parent, CNNMoney, and currently syndicates his writing and video blogs at Huffington Post and The Street. Most recently, he began an advice column at the business destination BNET.

I was delighted when Stanley agreed to be interviewed for this book.

* * *

Why did you start writing your column in Esquire?
I had a contact at Esquire and I was invited to write a column on business. I think I was the only guy they knew who worked in an office. At that time, I was working for Westinghouse, which became the CBS Corporation in 1997. I was just a guy off the street, an actor and a writer. At first, Westinghouse seemed to be a highly structured, hierarchical organisation made up of people who appeared to be serious doing serious work.

But, although the business world had pretensions to being otherwise – a pretension strengthened by business schools and publications that celebrated the man in the grey suit - Westinghouse was a place of aberrant, highly personalised behavior. The people at the top were the most pathological, and the ones at the bottom the most desperate, just as they were in journalism and the theatre. Business wasn't something carried out by people in a weird pod on the Planet Mambo, because ultimately, any kind of labour is about relationships and politics. You have to work with people and you have to figure them out.

My own business career as I progressed through Westinghouse fed the columns I wrote for Esquire. I wanted both to explain and make fun of business, so I'd write about things like the best way to make a business call or how to conduct a working relationship with a female boss if you were a man. I started at the back of the magazine, with The Strategist, and then moved to the front where I wrote longer, more general pieces. I wrote for Esquire for 11 years.

Do you think the corporate world is still sexy for young people coming out of college?
Today's corporate world is sexier than in the '80s. Men and women are working in a highly pressurised environment and there's the presence of money. Money is the ultimate sexiness for people in capitalism. It's sexier than sex. And people look good. Even people who go to work wearing hoodies make sure these are clean; and if they have stubble, they only have a day's growth. The corporate world will always be sexy because it's a place where people are doing and looking their best and making money.

And there are still lots of interesting businesses – startups, electronic communications, the Internet. They're snazzy and attractive. The bullshit's still the same, though.

What do you think about the idea of changing employment models – the trend for working remotely, for instance, which is happening in a big way in the US?

I was one of the first people to make fun of working from home, in a Fortune magazine column. I described my working days as shower, coffee, check email, go shopping, take lunch, maybe do some work. It's a kind of spasmy working. Although some functions can be done from home, I think groups are necessary. Business ideas start out wafer thin and they have to be battered against the wall by a group until they take on substance. And I'm not so sure big projects like bringing a product to market can be done remotely.

I believe Marisa Mayer of Yahoo had a point because I don't believe important, dynamic organisations can be made out of people just working remotely. Obviously, what she said hit a nerve with women who've fought hard to create a work-life balance that enables them to be with their families more.

But there was truth in what she said. Also, when it comes to letting people go it's the faces in front of the boss who are going to be kept on. And, if you're at home sleeping with your wife while I'm in the basement rowing the ship, I want to be saved before you are.

How do you see the cloud?
For a start, it's not a cloud; it's just one big, fat hard drive. Or a bunch of them. And they're highly vulnerable. If I were a terrorist I'd knock out a cloud server. And then there's changing weather - in Japan or on the East and West Coasts of America, for example. How far is the Google server from the San Andreas fault? The loss of everything stored in the cloud could be the modern equivalent of the destruction of the library at Alexandria. So I'm skeptical.

Do you think a cloud-based business like UP could succeed?
If it was a certain kind of business, like marketing communications, and it had a clear mission, yes. If there were a solid core of contributors to the business and enough of a hierarchy to create loyalty of function and spirit, and if the business had a clear vision, why not? Obviously, you'd have to limit the people who became part of the community – no whackos.

But you'd still need physical spaces for members of the organisation to meet and to be able to meet clients physically, face to face. If you could do that and work in the cloud, I could see it working.

Thanks Stanley, and to your last point, the next chapter.

> *There is no elevator to success. You have to take the stairs*
>
> *Unknown*

Chapter #11

Creative Spaces

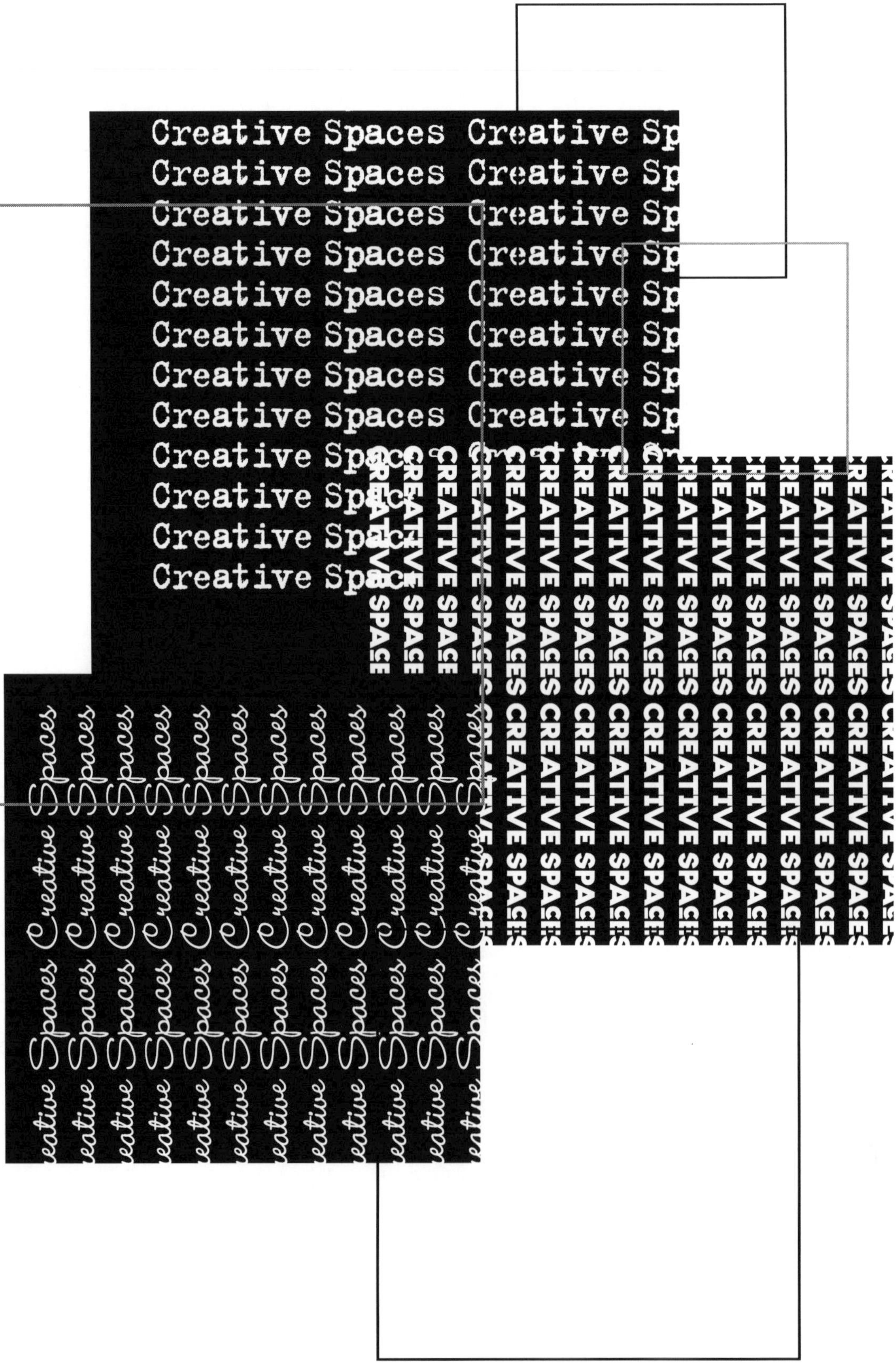
Creative Spaces
CREATIVE SPACES
Creative Spaces

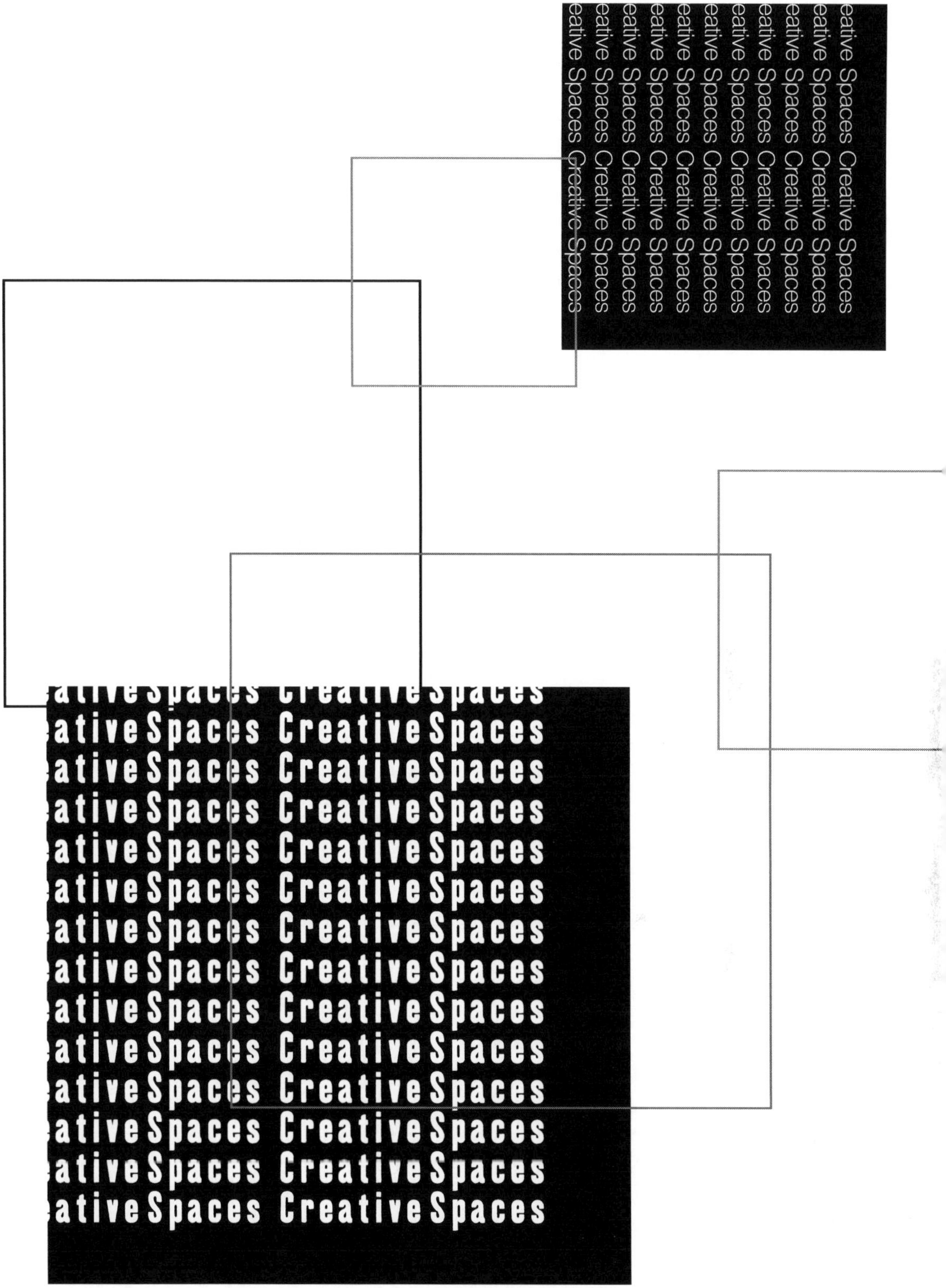
eative Spaces Creative Spaces
ative Spaces Creative Spaces

Two years after Eric and I had those conversations in the park that led to the creation of UP, we were once again in New York together. Only now things were very different.

* * *

The fall-out from the financial crisis, governments finding ways to limit spending and the constant evolution of the cloud had led to an employment landscape that was radically different from when UP was just a gleam in our eyes.

More and more people in the Western World were becoming self-employed, partly because they required more independence in their working lives, but also because they had no choice.

In our industry, this had led to the rise of so-called "talent exchange" sites that put clients together with self-employed, freelance writers, designers, programmers and so on. You already know my thoughts on this subject.

The concept behind UP was very different, and in the time since we had launched we'd had the opportunity to establish our own unique selling proposition. And our mantra was "people to people to people". We also had a unique methodology that I'd developed, that we called BASE-UP™, an acronym, that stood for: Brief, Audit, Strategy, Execution and follow UP. We liked it, and clients seemed to love it, because it was a methodical, step by step, approach that enabled us to deliver exactly the right strategy and creative solution.

People to People to People
The world has changed and changed radically during the past few years. The days of mass, impersonal, broadcast communications are over. We are all now more connected than ever before. And as individuals we are in control of what we want to see, experience and respond to. The conversation has become one to one. It's no longer business to consumer or business to business. It's people to people to people. It's human, it's emotional, it's personal.

And the clients we work together with want great people. Great people to work alongside them in true collaboration - because it's great people that create great ideas and ultimately great work. People working together.

That same focus, on people, goes to the very heart of UP and the simple idea and purpose that drives us. It's about breaking down the walls of the traditional ways of doing things. It's about supporting each other as people - the people who live and work within the UP community and organisation. People who work together everyday right around the world, enabled by the digital tools that have changed the way we live and work in the 21st century.

UP. It's about people.
Inevitably, more and more marketing communications companies in the West will set out their stall as "cloud-based". It will be the obvious thing to do. When we came up with UP, I'd say that Eric and I were just two reasonably smart people responding to the zeitgeist, and it is hardly surprising that other people will see the way the wind is blowing. Ultimately, though, we are delighted to be part of a movement, because it is proving to be the right thing to do and I'm proud that we are among the first to move our industry into the cloud.

* * *

No offices. Creative Spaces.
August in New York, and although it was early evening it was still hot and steamy, so Eric and I were sitting in the shade in the outside atrium of the Hudson Hotel, thinking about what was next for UP. We'd just launched in New York and opened a Creative Space on Broadway in SoHo, our second after Stockholm.

We'd always known that we would need a space to meet clients and have internal get-togethers as we expanded. We always knew that we hated (and I don't use that word very often in my life) going to "the office". I'd always seen offices as a means of boxing people in. Going to "the office" is a routine that too many people in the world have to follow that is completely unproductive for people in the creative services industry. Today we have over 150 people within UP. The thought of 150 people having to make the trek into a place, burning fuel, churning out CO_2 and burning time horrifies me. As the late Ian Dury said, "What A Waste".

However Eric and I also knew that, from time to time, various members liked the sense of structure that came with going to a space to work when needed, especially if it was a team session. Various factors had driven the rapid rise of hubs, and it was second nature for UP members to use them when we were on the move, when we were in "digital nomad" mode. Eric and my logic was, if we were all going to be using hubs and similar spaces, why not make them UP places wherever and whenever we could? We see them as Creative Spaces. Places where you go when needed for interaction. Not an office.

In the time since UP had been just a gleam in our eyes, more and more people had opened up these kinds of spaces. Some commentators claimed they were revolutionising how we worked. Maybe.

But we remained adamant that there would never be any such thing as an UP "office". The thought of it makes me shudder. For me, it's about thinking of work purely and simply as an activity. (22)

An incredibly capable woman named Kate Adams with a fantastic track record had just joined UP as Managing Director and we'd spent all day planning for the future.

"We're on the way", I said to Eric. "It's time for UP 2.0".

Eric nodded and smiled. "So, the experimental bit is over"?

"Yep. This is when it really starts to happen. Creative Spaces in New York and Stockholm, over 150 members of UP spread out all over the world, really high calibre people working with us, specialist groups like UP FOR GOOD (our sustainability and non-profit group), UP FOR LIFE (our life science and medical device group), UP FOR REAL (our place and destination branding group) and UP FOR IT (our technology group). And this was just the beginning".

"What next"? Eric asked.

"I'm hungry. Shall we eat"? I said.

Eric sighed. "No. I meant what next for UP"?

Which started me thinking.

* * *

Remember in Chapter One, where I talked about my early days in the wonderful world of work? How I dreamed of being the CEO of Julian Stubbs Inc.? When I was starting out, being self-employed - really employing your self - wasn't so common, at least in the UK, and young people like myself struggled to find a sense of direction.

Today, as we've seen, it's increasingly the case that people are becoming self-employed wherever they can. But what about all the young people facing a future in which it's becoming more and more difficult even to enter the world of work, let alone find something you really want to do?

Of course, there are young people like amazing 28-year-old Swedish entrepreneur Ulrika Bergenkrans, interviewed in this book, who possess the qualities of independence, determination and sheer talent that enable them to strike out on their own. But what about those who don't necessarily want to become self-employed right away, and who can't find a way into their chosen industry? What about the young people who don't live in a country like Sweden with a reasonably strong economy?

Young people could strategically relocate or, as an 80s UK politician Norman Tebbitt said, "get on their bike". In places like Spain, where UP has members, this has been happening for quite some time. Young Spanish people are heading for places like Germany and the UK (and even India!) to find work commensurate with their skills and qualifications. Or, in some cases, just any kind of work.

But, inevitably, the migration of young people tears the heart out of the communities from which they come. And, as I have made clear in previous chapters, I believe community is vital to a society's health.

***

In December 2013 I had been invited to give a speech about Place Branding at a conference held in the small Swedish town of Arjeplog, which lies just below the polar circle in Swedish Lapland. Arjeplog is the place where, in the middle of winter, the German, Italian and now the south Korean car industry test their new cars. Brand new, and sometimes un-launched, Porsches, Ferraris and Bentleys line up at the local fuel station to fill up. It's an incredible sight. They have even built a replica of Silverstone, the UK racetrack, on the ice. The population of the town doubles in the winter, as 2,500 engineers descend on the town. I sat by the mayor at dinner and she explained how this small town, despite the welcome seasonal influx from the car industry, is still struggling with de-population though. People, especially young people, leave for the big cities in the south. It made me realise that with more people having the capability to be "cloud-based" small remote locations, like Arjeplog, could find new ways to retain people and survive.

Our model could change the dynamic of remote places becoming desolate, and in fact they could become more appealing because of their remote location, slower pace of life and often lower cost of living. These are some of the elements that appeal to the so called Creative Class and it's an interesting thought.

So what other ways can we keep our talented young people in their own countries and communities? I started to think about internships.

In advertising, marketing and other branches of the media, internships are a standard method of entry into the industry. That is, if you can be accepted into an internship. They're highly sought after and, in many instances, it's still a case of who you know rather than... (you know the rest). Which means that plenty of talented people don't ever get the chance to show what they can do. And, without mentioning any names, some big media companies view interns as a disposable source of unpaid labour.

As I emphasised in the previous chapter, UP members are very experienced, which is great because we are skilled and knowledgeable and we have all been successfully self-employed for a number of years. We're the people for whom the system pretty much works. But, like all agencies and all organisations, UP needs new blood, especially digital natives, to grow and succeed.

When I was thinking this through, I realised that we were in the ideal position to offer a totally new kind of internship to talented people anywhere in the world. A cloud-based internship.

Why? Because that way we could offer bright, driven young people the opportunity to learn about and engage with marketing communications at a pretty sophisticated level without having to worry about the cost involved in moving to a new city, travel and so on. They didn't have to leave their families and communities unless they really wanted to. They could also offer their own entrepreneurial skills backed by all of the global resources of UP whenever they spotted an opportunity.

And, the great thing is that this applies as much for African countries, India or other developing countries as it does to young people in the traditional Western media centres like New York and London. This idea is something I really want to pursue as we grow UP. Maybe we should call it Growing UP.

"Sounds good", Eric said, when I told him that one of the things I wanted to do next was focus on recruiting more young people.

"What about you"? I asked.

* * *

As technologically savvy as he is, Eric hadn't fully realised the challenges involved in administering a global communications company solely using the cloud. To be fair, I certainly hadn't.

Once Eric and the other members of the team involved in building the UP administrative and finance system (our so-called SUPER System) had mapped it out functionally, it occurred to Eric that there was absolutely no reason why we couldn't offer it to other organisations that were considering moving into the cloud. We'd invested a cool quarter of a million dollars in it, so why not generate some revenue from it?

We'd believed for a long time that the UP model was perfect for other service industries and areas of business like accounting, architecture, financial services and the legal profession. Now we could offer them our system. And we were already talking to people in these industries who were like-minded.

There was also nothing to stop us from offering our expertise and systems to social enterprises, charities and other organisations trying to make a positive difference anywhere in the world.

This was part of Eric's vision and I shared it.

* * *

It was twilight when Eric and I strolled out of the hotel and down Broadway, one of my favourite streets in the world. The Great White Way is constantly buzzing. Whenever I'm in New York and it's a summer evening I always think of one particular line from F. Scott Fitzgerald's line in The Great Gatsby: "He wouldn't have been surprised to see a great flock of white sheep turn the corner".

A stoplight changed to green and we stepped onwards into the future of UP.

E-Ployment in essence:

E-Ployment is a new and evolving way of working and living for people in the service industries.

The key characteristics of E-Ployment are:

1. Gives you the ability to take full control of your own life.
2. Provides the flexibility to work where and when you want.
3. E-Ployment is enabled by digital, cloud based tools and systems.
4. E-Ployees will increasingly form and work in highly connected "communities".
5. E-Ployees will have the ability to work globally as well as locally.
6. E-Ployees will often derive their income from multiple sources and clients.
7. E-Ployees are more focussed on achieving a healthy work / life balance.
8. But E-Ployment demands greater self-responsibility.

Interview with Ulrika Bergenkrans
by David Holzer, UP member

She'll probably be embarrassed to read this but Ulrika is a remarkable 28-year old woman. Ulrika heads up TMM Ventures, based in Stockholm and, as well as being an entrepreneur, she's a marketing strategist and writer. She's also the co-founder of a lobbying organisation set up to win equal rights for women entrepreneurs.

I first heard about Ulrika when she was the face of a Swedish 'work from home' day in early 2013 promoted by the government and supported by Microsoft. I wanted to find out what a young Swedish person thought about new ways of working, including UP.

I talked to Ulrika at Café Espresso House on Stureplan, a bustling coffee shop and one of her favourite places to meet in downtown Stockholm.

* * *

How did you become an entrepreneur?
I started at university when I developed a website to earn extra income. Today I'm a general agent for two products: a sophisticated fertility monitor for women and a new type of sanitary product.

You strike me as very enterprising. Do you see yourself that way?
Maybe I am but, then, so are all my friends. I see a pattern among us. Many of us started out on a conventional career path. I worked for a PR company advising clients on digital and social media. But, after a year or two, quite quickly really, we started to wonder, "why am I working here 9-to-5 or, more likely, 9-to-1 in the morning"? And why do I have to submit to corporate policy? A lot of my friends have, like me, quit jobs and gone freelance. They've started their own businesses or are talking about it.

I see a new kind of courage and confidence among young Swedish people. Where do you think that comes from?
We were brought up in quite a stable time, historically. Our parents had to fight more for high material standards or even just to put food on the table. We saw our parents slave away. Many of us hardly saw our dads.

My generation, both in Sweden and across Scandinavia, is transitioning to a more entrepreneurial culture. We've gone from a very industrial segment to services because we don't have industry any more. There's a certain vitality right now, a Scandinavian energy. Maybe it has to do with the economic climate: we have to survive.

We have less fear. We feel we can leave one job if it's not working out and find another. There are more options on the market, always something new. The job we're in is not our last chance.

Are ethics in business important to you?
Yes, extremely. People my age are very hardworking, very loyal, they give their souls. But if we don't feel ourselves developing, if we don't get something back – flexibility and freedom, for example – we'll start to look around.

Beyond that, many things in the world concern me, mostly to do with gender equality.

How do you feel about the online world?
I got my first computer when I was ten or eleven, so I grew up with it and we've evolved together. My generation has a foot in both worlds, traditional and online, but my younger cousins grew up with Facebook and Twitter.

I have more of a physical need for meetings than people totally brought up in the digital world. I use social media tools, but physical meetings are very important for me.

What did you like about working in an office?
It was great for meetings and networking, being in the same room and making an idea grow. You can express yourself in so many different ways, unlike in chat rooms, on Skype or in a video conference.

What didn't you like?
I've always been a free spirit. I like to organise my own time. I want to have a task and feel free to accomplish it however I want. It's the modern way. There's no room for freedom and flexibility in the office. You sit your place between 9 am and 6 pm. If you're more effective after 7PM or in the early morning you're not allowed to be. The office felt very old-fashioned and restricted, and the philosophy around work showed a lack of trust.

How did you end up in Metro, the free Stockholm newspaper, as the face of "work from home" day?
I have a friend who works for Microsoft. I think it's a good initiative and I wanted to support it. It symbolises a more modern take on work generally.

How do you feel working from home affects productivity?
It's not just whether you work from home or anywhere else, like in a coffee shop. You have to be in that place for a reason. So, for instance, I want to work from home when I have copy to write. I can put my headphones on, be alone and no one can disturb me. Here, at the coffee shop, I can have meetings.

What do you think about online communities?
I'm a member of Facebook, Twitter, LinkedIn and Instagram. They're just channels, but I'm also a member of some of the online PR networks. These are not just online but physical also. Many communities like these are channels that help people meet.

What do you think about the UP idea?
Work has always been black and white – you either worked in traditional spaces or not. The UP concept is very interesting, very modern and different. It's like the way I'm doing business now but in an organised form, with the possibility to work with really good teams of people and backed by a strong brand. UP fits with the general outlook in Sweden, certainly among my generation, which wants a new way of working.

Epilogue

July 4th, 2013

Epilogue

It's the Fourth of July 2013, U.S. Independence Day, my wedding anniversary, and four years since I'd finally owned up to the fact that I needed to change my work life and my life life. Where am I? I'm in Amsterdam preparing to give a keynote speech on city and place marketing at the I amsterdam Partner Marketing day. (24) About 500 people sit expectantly in their seats, and I'm UP on stage next. The speech is being filmed as well, always an extra challenge as my jacket pockets are stuffed with various microphone transmitters. The audience includes several colleagues from UP, the global cloud-based agency that has taken shape out of what was no more than a vision three years before.

Thanks to Niki, whose advice gave me that wake-up call about my health, I'm in pretty good shape even if I let things slide a little from time to time. So, given that I'm in Holland making a presentation and not Sweden, and not having a candlelit dinner for two in a nice Stockholm restaurant with my wife, what conclusions would you draw about my work-life balance?

To be honest, it was when I understood that work-life balance wasn't about time but satisfaction I knew I had to make profound changes. As long as I ringfence the really important things in my work life and my life life, I no longer feel the need to try to divide the two. I know that for me it's about enjoying what I do, whenever and wherever I do it. I know it's also about stepping out of my own comfort zone and routines as often as possible, as this always makes me feel more fulfilled and like I'm growing. And it's the same for you, right? Above all, the most important thing for me and my fellow UP-members (and our clients) is our independence, and I'm eternally grateful that I've found a way to enable this.

I'm in a city that I enjoy and in the company of people who've become friends as much as colleagues – bright, like-minded people with whom I'm proud to share my journey. I'd say that, although we've a long way to go with UP, things are looking pretty good right now.

And if I've been able to plant the idea in your mind that a third way of living and working – in communities on- and off-line – makes sense, this book has done part of its job well.

It's my turn to speak. I step UP onto the stage and I'm off and running.

(To see my actual presentation search my name on You Tube).

e-ployment

Sources

Sources

When I was writing E-ployment, I was inspired by many different writers and thinkers who I discovered on and offline.

1. Roger B Hill's PhD thesis *Historical Context of the Work Ethic* proved invaluable in writing this chapter.
2. I came across the term "digital nomads" in an article on BBC Capital. It's a great term.
3. From Chris Ward's eye-opening and entertaining book *Out of Office*.
4. Leah Busque writing on Huffington Post.
5. Thanks to Mark Curtis for permission to quote from *Distraction: Being Human in the Digital Age*
6. A Stanford University study of 249 workers at a Chinese travel agency (*Does working from home work? Evidence from a Chinese Experiment* by Nicholas Bloom, James Lian, John Roberts, Zhichun Jenny Ying) coincidentally released around the same time of the Mayer Memo, evaluated workers who were randomly selected to work from home four days a week for nine months. The workers experienced a 13% increase in work performance.

    "The improvement came mainly from a 9 percent increase in the number of minutes worked during their shifts due to a reduction in breaks and sick-days taken. The remaining 4 percent came from an increase in the number of calls home workers took per minute worked, compared with those in the control group who weren't selected to work at home.

    Home workers also had more job satisfaction and were also less likely to quit their positions during the study. And the company saved about $2,000 per year for each employee who worked at home. (Reduced cost is one of the reasons federal agencies such as the National Institutes of Health have strongly encouraged employees to work at home at least one day each week.)"
7. One of these was Forbes.com contributor Carmine Gallo.
8. John Horn and Darren Pleasance, "Restarting the US small-business growth engine" McKinsey & Company, www.mckinsey.com/insights, November 2012.
9. Sale, Kirkpatrick, *Are Anarchists Revolting?*, The American Conservative
10. Fred Turner, *From Counterculture to Cyberculture*.
11, 12, 13. Scott Charles, *The Hyperink Thomas Friedman Quicklet Bundle*.
14. *History of Online Communities – DRAFT*: Preece, J., Maloney-Krichmar, D. and Abras, C. (2003) Karen Christensen &DavidLevinson (Eds.) is a great little potted history of the Internet.
15. Fred Turner, *From Counterculture to Cyberculture*.
16. In an interview with Carole Cadwalladr, *The Observer*, Sunday 5 May, 2013.
17. From blog.leadernetworks.com.
18. I'm grateful for the insight and inspiration offered by Jono Bacon in his ebook *The Art of Community* and, of course, Wikipedia.
19. Coined by writer and thinker M. Scott Peck
20. *Bowling Alone: The Collapse and Revival of American Community*.
21. When it came to researching this chapter, Richard gave generously of his time and his way of approaching business is both challenging and illuminating. I'm grateful to Richard for the insights his work has given me, and I strongly recommend that you visit newleadershipparadigm.com and take his free Personal Values Assessment test to explore what's important to you and makes you happy. Richard's books include The *New Leadership Paradigm and Liberating the Corporate Soul*. His latest book is The *Values-driven Organisation: Unleashing Human Potential for Performance and Profit*.
22. Thanks to Dave Coplin, Microsoft UK's chief envisioner, for this key insight.
23. I agree with Matthew Kelly, author of *Off Balance: Getting Beyond the Work-Life Balance Myth to Personal and Professional Satisfaction*, who says that being satisfied professionally and personally is more important than being balanced. For Matthew, the term "work-life balance" is fatally flawed because work and life are too intertwined.
24. You can see my July 4th speech on YouTube at:
    http://www.youtube.com/watch?v=4cwydikUL5g)

About the author
Julian Stubbs is a brand strategist, writer and presenter who has worked with developing brand strategies and identities for a wide range of organisations and places. From *Technicolor*, the Hollywood movie company to the *Nobel Peace Prize Concert*, to the city of *Stockholm*, in Sweden.

His first business book, titled *Wish You Were Here*, explores the branding of places and destinations as well as his work for the city of Stockholm, where Julian created the brand positioning and tag line "*Stockholm, The Capital of Scandinavia*". Today Julian is working with a number of place branding projects at city level and lecturing on the subject of Place Branding. He has most recently been involved with the city of Amsterdam, Liverpool and the city of Oslo.

He is a founder and CEO of **UP THERE, EVERYWHERE** the global cloud based consultancy group which today has over 150 people based in 19 cities around the world.

Julian travels about 100 days a year from his home just outside of Stockholm, Sweden. He is married with two boys and in his free time his passion is watching Liverpool football club, playing tennis, reading history and walking his Spanish water dog, whose name is London.

Wish You Were Here, which covers Place Branding and the branding work for Stockholm, is available on Amazon.com

> *We should never forget that we live in a real world of real people in real communities on a real planet that we need to look after. Working in the cloud means not having to commute to offices, being able to get our work-life balance right for the benefit of our families, and the communities we're part of, and living where and how we want to. It's long been recognised that mobility is a key generator of wealth*

Robert England
Early UP member, PhD and leader of
UP FOR LIFE, our life science and medical device team.

Printed in Great Britain
by Amazon.co.uk, Ltd.,
Marston Gate.